KÖNIGS ERLÄUTERUNGEN
Band 58

Textanalyse und Interpretation zu

William Shakespeare

RICHARD III

Patrick Charles

Analyse | Interpretation in englischer Sprache

Zitierte Ausgabe:
Geisen, Herbert: *William Shakespeare. King Richard III*. Reclam XL Englisch.
Reclams Universal Bibliothek Nr. 19961. Ditzingen: Reclam jun. Verlag, 2019.

Über den Autor dieser Erläuterung:
Patrick Charles wurde 1973 in Bournemouth, Südengland, geboren und studierte englische Literatur an der Universität von Newcastle. 1993 zog er nach Berlin, wo er eine Ausbildung zum Buchhändler machte und zehn Jahre lang als Buchhändler arbeitete. Seit 2004 ist er als freiberuflicher Autor von Schulbüchern und Lernhilfen und als Übersetzer im Kulturbereich tätig. Er lebt mit seiner Familie in Berlin.

1. Auflage 2020
ISBN: 978-3-8044-2053-3
PDF: 978-3-8044-6053-9, EPUB: 978-3-8044-7053-8
© 2020 by Bange Verlag GmbH, 96142 Hollfeld
Alle Rechte vorbehalten!
Titelabbildung: picture alliance / Photoshot
Druck und Weiterverarbeitung: Tiskárna Akcent, Vimperk

CONTENT

1. AT A GLANCE — 6

2. WILLIAM SHAKESPEARE: LIFE & WORK — 9

2.1 Biography — 9
2.2 Contemporary Background — 11
Politics and society — 11
Culture and the theatre — 14
Niccoló Machiavelli — 15
2.3 Notes on Other Important Works — 16
The tragedies — 16
The comedies — 18
The history plays — 19
The sonnets — 21

3. ANALYSES AND INTERPRETATIONS — 23

3.1 Origins and Sources — 23
Historical sources — 23
Artistic sources – Senecan tragedy — 24
3.2 Summaries — 27
Act I — 27
Act II — 30
Act III — 32
Act IV — 35
Act V — 38
3.3 Structure — 40
3.4 Characters — 43
Main characters – House of York — 44

Richard, later King Richard III	44
King Edward IV	47
George, Duke of Clarence	48
Duchess of York	48
Queen Elizabeth	48
The young Prince Edward	49
The young Duke of York	49
Boy and Girl	49
The Woodvilles	50
Marquess of Dorset	50
Lord Grey	50
Earl Rivers	50
Women of the House of Lancaster	50
Old Queen Margaret	50
Lady Anne	51
Other nobles	52
Earl of Richmond (Henry Tudor)	52
Lord Hastings	54
Lord Stanley	55
Supporters of Richard	56
Duke of Buckingham	56
Sir Richard Ratcliff	57
Sir William Catesby	57
Lord Lovel	57
Sir Robert Brakenbury	58
Earl of Surrey	58
Duke of Norfolk	58
Further characters	58
3.5 Notes on themes	61
The history plays: genre and themes	61
The themes of *Richard III*	64

Morality, immorality and the laws	64
Ambition & power	69
3.6 Style and language	**81**
Rhetoric	81
Black comedy	83
Boar imagery	85
Extreme language and imagery	86
3.7 Interpretations	**88**
Power and manipulation	88
Al Pacino's *Looking for Richard*	89

4. RECEPTION 91

5. MATERIALS 94

The Globe Theatre in London — 94
Some useful information — 96

6. SAMPLE EXAM QUESTIONS AND ANSWERS 98

SOURCES & REFERENCES 101

INDEX 103

1. AT A GLANCE

This study guide to William Shakespeare's play *Richard III* is designed to provide an easy-to-use overview of the structure, context, themes and characters of the play. Here is a quick rundown of the most important points.

> **Citations:** When quoting from the play or referring to specific passages, the following reference is used: Act II Scene 4 lines 55–57 is written II.4.55–57. So III.1.67–74 refers to Act III, Scene 1, lines 67 to 74.

Part 2 takes a brief look at **Shakespeare and his career**.

⇨ p. 9
- → **Shakespeare was born in Stratford-upon-Avon** in the county of Warwickshire (England) in 1564. Around 1585 he began to act, produce plays and write for the stage.

⇨ p. 11
- → ***Richard III*** (ca. 1593) is one of the longest plays Shakespeare ever wrote. Its **relevance to the political climate of his era** – Tudor monarchy – made it popular with contemporary audiences.

⇨ p. 16
- → Most of **his work was written in the years 1589–1613**. Shakespeare achieved success and critical acclaim during his lifetime, and he was one of the most prominent writers of his era. His plays are usually categorised as **comedies, tragedies or history plays**.

Part 3 provides analyses and interpretations of the play.

Richard III – Origins and Sources:

⇨ p. 23
Shakespeare took his material from chronicles of English history. He adapted it to suit his artistic goals. But Shakespeare was primarily a

poet and not a historian, so here – as in his other history plays – he happily bent and manipulated the historical facts to suit his poetic and artistic purpose. *Richard III* was probably written in 1593.

Summaries:

Richard III is about Richard Duke of Gloucester, a physically and morally deformed man who is determined to become King of England, by any means necessary. He sets out with a few allies to spread rumours about anyone who opposes him or stands between him and the throne. He has already begun to murder his opponents before the play begins. For Richard, loyalty is a one-way street, and he repeatedly sacrifices and eliminates supposed allies and followers when it suits him. Once he has seized the throne, however, Richard begins to fall apart, becoming steadily more paranoid as he faces an increasingly powerful and righteous rebellion. He is eventually slain on the battlefield by Richmond, bringing an end to the traumatic civil wars known as the *Wars of the Roses*.

⇨ p. 27

Structure:

Richard III is **a five-act play**. The dramatic structure follows a classic pattern of Introduction – Rising action – Climax – Falling action – Catastrophe and resolution.

⇨ p. 40

Characters:

The play is about the warring dynasties of noble houses in England during the 15th century. The cast of characters is long and can be very confusing. Here are the most important characters:

- → **Richard, Duke of Gloucester, later King Richard III.** The protagonist und absolutely dominant figure in the play. ⇨ p. 44
- → His brothers **King Edward IV and George, Duke of Clarence**. ⇨ p. 47
- → The **Duchess of York**, their mother ⇨ p. 48

⇨ p. 48	→ **Queen Elizabeth**, wife/widow of King Edward IV
⇨ p. 50	→ Old **Queen Margaret**, widow of King Henry VI: She curses Richard and his followers.
⇨ p. 51	→ **Lady Anne**, daughter-in-law of Queen Margaret, later Richard's wife
⇨ p. 52	→ **Earl of Richmond**, Henry Tudor: Richmond kills Richard in battle.
⇨ p. 56	→ **The Duke of Buckingham:** A loyal and extremely useful ally to Richard during his climb to power.

Themes:

⇨ p. 61

The major themes we will look at in this study guide are morality, immorality and the moral law of the Tudor universe: ambition, power and the abuse of power; and fate, free will and fatalism.

Style and Language:

⇨ p. 81

The language of the play, Shakespeare's poetic Elizabethan English, can be hard to understand and follow. The stylistic tools we will look at here are rhetoric and black humour.

Interpretation

⇨ p. 88

Richard III has remained a popular play with audiences. It has also proved to have lasting and consistent relevance to any society in any era. The core subject matter of an illegitimate and morally unfit leader, like Richard, speaks to all audiences. Wherever there are large groups of people, there are those who seek power, and amongst those there will probably be at least a few budding Richards. The political and moral content of the play will continue to keep audiences fascinated.

2. WILLIAM SHAKESPEARE: LIFE & WORK

2.1 Biography

Much of Shakespeare's life is documented, in particular after he began to have success as a playwright. Not everything is relevant to the study of an individual play: here are some of the most important landmarks in Shakespeare's life. More specific information about his plays and his career can be found in the chapter on Other Works (see page 16), and the chapter on Contemporary Background (p. 11) gives a broader context for his life and his plays.

William Shakespeare (1564–1616) © picture alliance / TopFoto

YEAR	PLACE	EVENT	AGE
1564	Stratford-upon-Avon, England	Probably born on April 23, baptized on April 26 in Stratford-upon-Avon, in the county of Warwickshire in England. He was the third of eight children.	
1582	Stratford-upon-Avon	Marries Anne Hathaway. They have three children.	18
1583	Stratford-upon-Avon	Baptism of the daughter Susanna	19
1585	Stratford-upon-Avon	Baptism of the twins Hamnet and Judith	21
1585–1592		The "lost years". Nothing is known about this period of Shakespeare's life. By the time he reappears in the historical records in 1592, he is living in London and has already written plays which have been performed on stage. He also regularly performs as an actor.	21–28

2.1 Biography

YEAR	PLACE	EVENT	AGE
1592	London	Shakespeare's name first appeared in print on the London theatre scene. Robert Green, a playwright, gets upset about a young upstart, "an upstart crow, beautified with our feathers"[1].	28
1593–1594	London	**Shakespeare writes *Richard III*.**	29–30
1594	London	From this year on, Shakespeare's plays were exclusively performed by the Lord Chamberlain's Men, a theatre company co-owned by Shakespeare.	30
1597	London	***Richard III* is published.**	33
1598	London	From this point onwards, Shakespeare had become successful enough that his name was used to advertise his works. ***Richard III* is probably first performed on stage.**	34
1599	London	Members of the Lord Chamberlain's Men worked together to establish the Globe theatre on the south bank of the River Thames.	35
1616	Stratford-upon-Avon	Shakespeare dies in Stratford-upon-Avon. The cause of death is unknown.	52
1623	London	*First Folio* published: First complete edition of Shakespeare's works.	

---

[1] Greenblatt, Stephen; Abrams, M. H.: *The Norton Anthology of English Literature. Volume I.* New York, London: Norton & Company, 2006. p. 1058.

2.2 Contemporary Background

2.2 Contemporary Background

> SUMMARY
>
> Shakespeare was born during the reign of Queen Elizabeth I. The age of her reign, the Elizabethan Age, is famous for the blossoming of the theatre – with playwrights William Shakespeare and Christopher Marlowe at its centre.

Politics and society

Shakespeare was born during the reign of Queen Elizabeth I (reigned 1558–1603). Elizabeth was the last of the monarchs of the **House of Tudor**. Elizabeth is one of the most famous rulers in British and English history: the time of her rule is widely referred to as **"the Elizabethan Age"** (the only other period in British and English history which is equally strongly characterised by the ruler is the rule of Queen Victoria, 1837–1901, called "the Victorian Age").

Elizabeth is a complex figure, but in general, her rule is seen in a positive light, **as she brought an important stability to the country,** which had long been caught in bloody conflicts between the major noble houses and dynasties, and which had also been torn apart by religious conflicts between Catholics (who acknowledged the Pope in Rome as their spiritual leader) and the newer Protestant forms of Christianity. Elizabeth was not a Catholic, and she followed her father, King Henry VIII, in forcing a more **liberal Protestant-influenced Anglican Church** catering specifically to British and English believers.

Queen Elizabeth I

Elizabeth's sister **Mary, Queen of Scots**, was a famously pious Catholic, which had led to a long history of complex and deadly intrigues and struggles between the sisters. The Protestant churches were determined to break away from the often corrupt rule of Rome,

Queen Mary

2.2 Contemporary Background

and insisted on, among other things, holding church services in the congregation's own language rather than in Latin, so that the uneducated masses could finally understand what they were hearing, and banning outright the utterly corrupt Catholic practice of allowing believers to literally purchase (with money) forgiveness for their sins.

"The Virgin Queen"

Queen Elizabeth I relied on advisors and was by all accounts an intelligent and conscientious woman. The age of her reign is most famous for the blossoming of the theatre – **this was the age of Shakespeare and Christopher Marlowe** – as well as the more controversial expansion of English power through the efforts of explorers (or to phrase it more honestly, state-sanctioned pirates) like Sir Francis Drake. The other lasting landmark of her rule was her **defeat of the Spanish Armada in 1588**, decisively and victoriously ending a long period of tension and conflict with an aggressive Spain.

As noted, Elizabeth was a Protestant ruler, and she had long been in conflict with her sister Mary, Queen of Scots, who was an ardent Catholic. **Elizabeth was relatively tolerant of other religious beliefs.** She was instrumental in establishing the Church of England, otherwise known as the Anglican Church, which kept some doctrine from Catholicism while rejecting the authority of Rome, and embracing the political and social implications of the Protestant Reformation.

England was, during **the time of Shakespeare**, caught between the major powers of the era – **France and Spain**. Both countries were larger, richer and more powerful than England. England had long had a complex, incestuous and conflicted history with France. The two countries are historically about as closely-connected as it is possible for two countries to be without sharing a common language. As well as some military squabbles over the French port

2.2 Contemporary Background

The "Armada-Portrait": Queen Elizabeth I (1533–1603), painted by George Gower.
© picture alliance/Photo12/Ann Ronan Picture Library

of Le Havre, the Elizabethan Age saw a number of small-scale English military adventures on French soil, all of which ended either pointlessly or disastrously.

During this period in history, it was very much on the seas and oceans of the world that England was able to establish itself as a **military power**. This naval power translated into increased political influence among the constantly squabbling states of Europe.

2.2 Contemporary Background

Culture and the theatre

As noted, this era and the one to follow – the reign of King James I (adjective: Jacobean) – was a landmark in the history of English literature and culture. Poetry and in particular **the stage drama** blossomed and developed in huge leaps during Elizabeth's reign, and continued to throw out new forms and themes and sources for stories and characters. The unquestionably dominant figure of this period was **William Shakespeare**, generally recognised as the greatest poet and dramatist in the history of English culture.

Christopher Marlowe

Shakespeare may have been a major force in literature, but he was not alone, and his talent did not emerge from or blossom in a vacuum. **Christopher "Kit" Marlowe** (1564–1593) was the most successful writer of tragedies for the stage before his mysterious murder at a young age. He achieved fame and respect before Shakespeare, even though they were the same age, and would have been an important role-model for Shakespeare as he was establishing himself as a playwright.

Literary critics have long been aware of the influence Marlowe had on Shakespeare, which included Shakespeare's use of "Marlowe's themes", most relevantly the artistic investigation of ambition and morality.

Marlowe had also made use of many different sources for his plays, such as the *German Faustbuch*, the original literary text concerning the legend of the scholar Faust and his deal with the devil Mephistopheles: Marlowe's *Doctor Faustus* (two versions from 1604 and 1616) was the first drama version of the legend, which was also of course adapted by Goethe over a century later in *Faust*.

2.2 Contemporary Background

Niccoló Machiavelli

A less direct but equally important influence on Shakespeare – and many others – was the text *The Prince*[2] (1513) by the Italian diplomat and writer Niccoló Machiavelli (1469–1527). Machiavelli was an **important influence on Marlowe**, who included the historical figure in at least one of his plays, and on any other writer to follow him who had even the slightest artistic interest in power and ambition as literary themes.

Machiavelli is most famous for his analysis of power and the means and methods of achieving, applying and maintaining it. He believed that **morality and moral considerations were irrelevant** and useless in this context. The matter of power was, he thought, more like a board game with rules based entirely around accomplishing the goal of "winning". The immoral methods that power-hungry men may use – deceit, assassination, corruption, invasion, etc. – are simply tools available for use by all involved; by all those who are playing the game.

The game of power

The relevance of this political philosophy to *Richard III* is immediately apparent. **Shakespeare's Richard is clearly Machiavellian** – he is willing to use any and every tool at his disposal to achieve power for himself, including the murder of children. The themes of ambition and power in *Richard III* will be looked at in more depth in the chapter in this study guide on Themes (p. 61).

---

2 Ital.: *Il Principe*.

2.3 Notes on Other Important Works

2.3 Notes on Other Important Works

SUMMARY

> Shakespeare wrote 39 plays (probably – there is some debate about whether this number is accurate). He also wrote poems, most importantly 154 sonnets.
> The plays were collected in 1623 in the "*First Folio*". The categorisation of the plays in tragedies, comedies and history plays begins with this collection. The *First Folio* remains the most important source for the texts of the plays.

The plays

Shakespeare's plays are traditionally categorised in three separate groups: **the tragedies, the comedies and the history plays**. This organisation is useful in addition to a basic chronological approach of his entire bibliography.

> **Note:** the dates of the plays' writing, publication and first performance are often approximate. The dates given here are the general consensus according to Shakespeare scholars.

The tragedies

What is a tragedy?

Tragedy is a dramatic structure which was as far as we know first developed by **the ancient Greeks**, and was later expanded upon and further explored by the Romans, in particular **Seneca** (4 BC–AD 65). Seneca's tragedies became a major, dominant influence on the rebirth of tragedy in Italy, France, Spain and Britain during the **Renaissance** of the 15th and 16th centuries (for more on this era and its relevance to Shakespeare, see the chapters in this study

2.3 Notes on Other Important Works

guide on Contemporary Background, p. 11 and Origins and Sources, p. 23).

Tragedy is most simply defined as a **drama based on human suffering** which causes pleasure in the audience. This pleasure – felt at the expense of the characters in the drama, in a way – has been the subject of philosophical and critical debate for centuries. One crucial concept here is **the idea of catharsis**.

> **Catharsis** (n., adj. chathartic) – defined by the *Oxford Advanced Learner's Dictionary* as "the process of releasing strong feelings, for example through plays or other artistic activities, as a way of providing relief from anger, suffering, etc."[3].
> The original term in ancient Greek means purification or cleansing. The idea was developed by Aristotle (384–322 BC). In drama, particularly in tragic drama, catharsis is interesting because it is functional – the cathartic drama and the audience in search of catharsis are collaborating in something which in many ways has more to do with religious or cult ritual than it has to do with what we would typically call "entertainment".

---

3 https://www.oxfordlearnersdictionaries.com/definition/english/catharsis?q=catharsis

2.3 Notes on Other Important Works

Shakespeare's tragedies:

TITLE	YEAR WRITTEN	PERFORMED
Antony and Cleopatra	1601–1608	1606–1608
Coriolanus	1605–1608	1682
Hamlet	1601	1602
Julius Caesar	1599	1599
King Lear	1603–1606	1606
Macbeth	1603–1606	1611
Othello	1602–1604	1604
Romeo and Juliet	1595–1596	1596
Timon of Athens	1607	1678
Titus Andronicus	1593	1594
Troilus and Cressida	1602	1609

The comedies

What is a comedy? A comedy is a work of art or entertainment which is intended to be **humorous or to provoke laughter**. As with tragedy, the roots of comedy lie in Ancient Greece.

Specific to Shakespeare's works and the Elizabethan era in which he lived and wrote, a comedy is a play with a **light tone and a happy ending** which almost always involved a marriage between as-yet unmarried characters. The comedies are less dark in tone and subject matter than the tragedies, as one would expect, and they sometimes contain elements of the fantastic, which are very rare in the history plays.

2.3 Notes on Other Important Works

TITLE	YEAR WRITTEN	PERFORMED
All's Well That Ends Well*	1598–1608	1623
As You Like It	1599	1603
The Comedy of Errors	1589–1595	1594
Love's Labour's Lost	Mid-1590s	Mid-1590s
Measure for Measure*	1604	1604
The Merchant of Venice	1596–1599	1605
The Merry Wives of Windsor	1597	1660
A Midsummer Night's Dream	1595–1596	1662
Much Ado About Nothing	1598–1599	Ca. 1598
Pericles, Prince of Tyre*	1607–1608	1608
The Taming of the Shrew	1590–1592	1594
The Tempest*	1610–1611	1611
Twelfth Night	1601–1602	1602
The Two Gentlemen of Verona	1589–1593	Before 1598
The Two Noble Kinsmen*	1613–1614	1613–1614
The Winter's Tale*	1610–1611	1611
Cymbeline*	Unknown	1611

* These plays are traditionally and typically grouped with the comedies, but they contain some elements which have led some Shakespeare scholars to refer to them as the **romances** or even the **problem plays**, and to draw attention to the ways in which they differ from the structures and themes of Shakespeare's comedies. Critics argue that the problem plays, for example, like *All's Well That Ends Well*, are concerned with more complex ethical conflicts than the comedies.

The history plays

These are plays which are based on historical sources. Specifically, they are **biographies of kings of England** from earlier centuries. The historical English subject matter is what defines this portion of Shakespeare's work, and it is what excludes other historically

Historical sources

2.3 Notes on Other Important Works

founded works like *Julius Caesar* (which is set in ancient Rome) and *Macbeth* (set in Scotland in the 11th century).

The play we are looking at, **Richard III**, is firmly situated among the history plays. In the first and most important publication of the plays, the **First Folio of 1623**, the history plays are sorted according to the historical chronology, rather than alphabetically or by date of composition. The list below follows this chronology:

TITLE	YEAR WRITTEN	PERFORMED	NOTES ON CHRONOLOGY
King John	1587–1598	1737	King John reigned 1199–1216.
Edward III	Before 1596	1598	King Edward III reigned 1327–1377.
Richard II	1595	1595	King Richard II reigned 1377–1399.
Henry IV, Part 1	Before 1597	1597	Covers the period 1402–1403.
Henry IV, Part 2	1596–1599	Before 1612	Follows on from Part 1 to the coronation of Henry V.
Henry V	1599	1599	Henry V reigned 1413–1422.
Henry VI, Part 1	1591	1592	These four plays belong together as they cover the years 1422 (the death of King Henry V) to 1485 (when Henry VII came to power). This period of war and conflict is known as the *Wars of the Roses*.
Henry VI, Part 2	1591	1592	
Henry VI, Part 3	1591	1592	
Richard III	1591–1593	1633	
Henry VIII	1613	1613	King Henry VIII reigned 1509–1547.

2.3 Notes on Other Important Works

The sonnets

Shakespeare wrote 154 sonnets, which were first collected and **published in 1609**. A sonnet is a strict form for poetry: it has 14 lines, with three quatrains and a couplet, and is written in iambic pentameter. The rhyme scheme is also strictly determined by the form.

Quatrains are verses of four lines.

A couplet is two lines in a poem which typically use the same rhythm and rhyme.

Iambic pentameter is the name given to a specific measurement of rhythm – this measurement is called the metre – which is used in a poem. Rhythm in poetry is measured in what are called "feet" – these are small groups of syllables. Iambic is a kind of foot (like a kilogramme is a kind of weight). An iambic foot is an unstressed syllable followed by a stressed syllable – for example, be-*neath* or be-*tray*. Pentameter – which means a measure (-meter) of five (penta-) refers to a line in a poem containing five feet.

The rhyme scheme describes the pattern of rhymes within the poem. Rhyme schemes are usually and very simply written using letters to signify which section rhymes with which – for a Shakespearean sonnet, the rhyme scheme is:

ABAB (the first quatrain: lines 1 and 3 rhyme, as do lines 2 and 4)
CDCD (the second quatrain)
EFEF (the third quatrain)
GG (the couplet)

> What does this all mean?

Shakespeare is credited with having revolutionised the sonnet's function as poetry by taking the **strict format and filling it with many new subjects**. Whereas sonnets – which for our purposes originated in Italy during the Renaissance – were nearly always poetic expressions of love for an unattainable, almost divinely desirable and beautiful woman, Shakespeare began to write about

> New topics

2.3 Notes on Other Important Works

many other topics. The object of the sonnet was no longer exclusively a beloved woman: now he was writing sonnets focussed on young men, women who were more dangerous than desirable, and on specific feelings and attitudes which were more complex and darker than poetic love, like infidelity, hatred and resentment.

3. ANALYSES AND INTERPRETATIONS

3.1 Origins and Sources

SUMMARY

Shakespeare writes *Richard III* around 1592/93. It is published in 1597 and first performed on stage in 1598. *Richard III* is grouped among the histories in the *First Folio*.

Historical sources

Shakespeare made good use of historical chronicles and other sources in writing his history plays. His *Richard III* is believed to have been developed from Thomas More's *History of King Richard III*, which he had read in chronicles compiled by **Edward Hall** (1542) and **Raphael Holinshead** (1577, revised in 1587)[4]. These two chroniclers – Hall and Holinshead – were evidently his favourite sources for historical matters, as he used them time and again for his history plays.

But we must always remember that Shakespeare's "history" plays were a living, relevant reminder or **memory of his contemporary political and social environment**. The *Wars of the Roses* were real history for Shakespeare's world, and that meant that there was a real political aspect to how these historical dramas could be told (for more on the contemporary and relevant historical background, see the chapter in this study guide on Contemporary Background, p. 11).

Wars of the Roses

This contemporary relevance of historical events meant that Shakespeare was sometimes more relaxed when it came to the ac-

---

[4] See introduction to *Richard III* in: Wells; Taylor: *William Shakespeare: The Complete Works*. p. 183.

3.1 Origins and Sources

curacy and truth of his historical subjects. **He was not a historian: he was a poet and playwright**. And he was not a rebel: he was the subject of a Tudor monarch. Therefore, we will often find with his historical plays that actual events and historical figures are modified to suit his needs as a storyteller and as a Tudor citizen.

Historical inaccuracies

Some of these historical inaccuracies concern the degree of Richard's villainy. As the last of the Plantagenet House of York monarchs, defeated by the House of Tudor, it was necessary that he be presented as a force of evil. Some of the murders attributed to Richard in Shakespeare's play were not actually committed or commissioned by **the real Richard**. He became Lord Protector by an Act of Parliament, not by means of devious murders and schemes. It is almost certainly not true that he intended to marry his niece – this was a rumour with no factual basis.

Shakespeare also compressed the timescale of the actual, historical events **into much shorter periods**: the story of Richard's ascent to the throne as described in the first half of the play lasted twelve years in reality, and it was two years after taking the crown that he was killed in battle[5].

Artistic sources – Senecan tragedy

Lucius Annaeus Seneca (ca. 4 BC – AD 65) was an ancient Roman philosopher, dramatist and politician. He established a particular type of dramatic tragedy which has become known as **Senecan tragedy.** This particular kind of drama was rediscovered centuries later by Italians in the 16th century, during the historical period known as the Renaissance (literally: rebirth).

---

5 Ibid., p. 183.

3.1 Origins and Sources

Senecan tragedy was highly influential in many different national and formal kinds of theatre, but what interests us most is its effect on **Elizabethan tragedy** – the world of Shakespeare's theatre.

Senecan tragedy took stories and figures from ancient Greek myths, but adapted these elements and the themes and ideas to explore Seneca's own philosophical ideas. The Senecan tragedy makes great **use of rhetoric** – characters arguing their points alone or with one another. The Senecan tragedy is further characterised by violence and the supernatural. The acts of violence may or may not be presented on stage, more often they are referred to or discussed, and the supernatural elements are typically ghostly.

Ancient Greek myths

Senecan rhetoric, abundant **acts of violence** and the **use of ghosts** are all familiar elements in Shakespeare's plays. The violence is more or less extreme, depending on the play – for example Shakespeare's earlier *Titus Andronicus* (written ca. 1593), believed to be his first tragedy, is also his most **violent and gruesome**, with horrific acts of violence being carried out onstage, rather than offstage, as in *Richard III*. Many contemporary plays, and in particular later plays from the "Revenge tragedy" genre during the reign of King James in the early 1600s, delighted in these gory spectacles. They can perhaps be compared to the modern appeal of bloody and brutal horror films (i.e., *The Evil Dead* 1981; *Saw* 2004) in which the violence and gore is itself part of the appeal, as opposed to less explicit, more unnerving horror (*Rosemary's Baby* 1968; *Don't Look Now* 1973) which focus less on the immediate threat of physical pain or damage to create a sense of dread and horror. Shakespeare's audiences would also have had the choice of wild, bloody spectacle in their drama, or subtler, rhetorical horror such as Richard murdering his way to the throne in *Richard III*.

Violence

The use of **supernatural elements** was very appealing because it allows the acts of the protagonists to in a way have a voice for

Supernatural elements

3.1 Origins and Sources

themselves: the ghosts of murdered rivals or innocents returning to curse, threaten or warn the protagonist represent the conscience – however deficient – of the main character, taking form onstage to show us, the audience, as well as the protagonist, what **the consequences of their evil actions** have been.

In *Richard III* we also have ghosts onstage, but here we have two opposing instances. Richard's ghosts are dark and frightening and curse him, but Richmond instead sees ghosts who bless his course and wish him well in his rebellion against the illegitimate and evil King Richard III.

3.2 Summaries

> King Edward's brother, Richard, begins to aspire to the throne and plans to kill anyone he has to in order to become king. First, he eliminates his brother Clarence to hasten Edward's death – then he kills a variety of other people to get to the throne.
> Finally, at Bosworth Field, Richard battles with Richmond. The night before, Richard has a terrible dream in which the ghosts of all the people he has murdered appear and predict Richard's death, and the next day, Richard is killed by Richmond. The war of the Lancaster and York houses is over.

SUMMARY

Act I
Act I Scene 1
In London, Richard, Duke of Gloucester, enters the stage alone. He explains how successful the house of York has been, emerging victorious from the recent conflicts in the country. The time of war and conflict has passed, he says, and people are now happy and celebrating. But Richard says that he is not designed for times of peace: being ugly and deformed and having a twisted and immoral sense of ambition, he sees no opportunities for himself and is determined to become a villain. He has begun laying plots against his brother Clarence and against King Edward.

Clarence enters the stage, under guard. He tells Richard that the king has ordered him to be imprisoned in the Tower of London. He tells Richard that the king is being influenced by rumours and prophecies. Richard says it is the king's wife, Lady Grey, who is behind the plot against Clarence. Richard tells Clarence before he

Clarence is arrested

3.2 Summaries

leaves under guard that he will intervene with the king to try to have his brother released.

Alone again, Richard bids farewell to Clarence, saying that he will soon be executed.

The Lord Chamberlain, Lord Hastings, now enters. He has been released from prison. He tells Richard that the king is weak and is dying and then exits.

Richard decides to go to the king to stir up hatred against Clarence, in order to have him executed more swiftly. In his plan, the king will soon die, leaving him, Richard, to seize power and make a politically advantageous marriage (to Lady Anne).

Act I Scene 2

Lady Anne and the dead King Henry VI

Lady Anne enters, accompanying the corpse of King Henry VI. She asks the pall bearers to set down the body so that she can mourn him. She curses the man who killed the king. When she is done, she asks the pall bearers to continue to their destination.

Then Richard enters and orders them to set the coffin back down. Anne is furious at him, cursing and insulting him. She accuses him of being a monster and of having murdered her intended husband. Richard claims he did not, telling her that it was Edward who killed him.

Richard argues against her by constantly complimenting her and mentioning her beauty. He seems to be courting her, and tells her that he loves her. She is horrified and basically says she would rather die than ever be close to him.

But Richard continues talking and claiming to love her and to feel repentant for all he has done. Anne's hatred and defiance weakens and she eventually agrees to marry him. She leaves, and Richard says that he has only been pretending to love her. He has begun making plans for his future.

3.2 Summaries

Act I Scene 3
The queen enters with Lord Rivers and Lord Grey, talking about the health of the king. Richard enters and accuses her of treachery: She in turn accuses him of being jealous of her and her friends and followers. Richard claims that true nobles are being imprisoned and punished while her followers, whom he says are less than noble, are being advanced and favoured.

While Richard is arguing with the queen and her followers, the old Queen Margaret enters. She speaks in asides (to the audience, rather than to other characters on stage), accusing Richard of having killed her husband and son. She calls him a devil. Eventually she can no longer stand the arguments and she approaches, attacking Richard. Richard reminds her that she has been banished on pain of death. She warns the other nobles gathered about Richard and his treacherous, murderous actions. She curses them, and they unite to defy her, calling her a lunatic, among other things. She predicts that they will regret having anything to do with Richard and that all will suffer (she exempts Buckingham from this curse): "The day will come that thou shalt wish for me / To help Thee curse this poisonous bunch-back'd toad." (l. 245+)

Queen Margaret warns about Richard

Margaret leaves and Richard makes a display of showing understanding and pity for her behaviour. Catesby then enters and summons the queen to see the king. All leave but Richard.

He speaks about how he uses morals and fake behaviour to mask his treachery and plotting. He meets with two murderers and orders them to kill Clarence.

Act I Scene 4
Clarence is in the Tower with a guard. Clarence describes a dream he has had. In the dream he has escaped from the Tower and is on a boat with Richard, bound for France. Richard stumbles and pushes

3.2 Summaries

Clarence into the water. While drowning in his dream, Clarence sees unimaginable wealth and riches scattered across the ocean floor. He dreams that he crosses the river of the dead into the underworld, where he encounters ghosts accusing him of treason. He is attacked by demons and ghosts and his terror awakens him. He tells the guard that he is exhausted and, with the guard watching over him, he sleeps.

Clarence is killed

The two murderers sent by Richard enter. The first is eager to kill Clarence, but the second is struggling with his conscience. Clarence awakes and realises they are here to kill him. He argues with them for his life and they tell him that Richard sent them, which he refuses to believe.

The first murderer stabs him and leaves with the body. The second murderer refuses to take part in the murder at all and leaves.

Act II
Act II Scene 1

In the palace in London: King Edward IV enters with the queen and other nobles. The king is sick, and he commands the nobles, who are rivals, to swear their love for one another before him. They all do so, including the queen. Their vows and promises are exaggerated and seem untrustworthy.

Richard enters. He also professes his love of peace and harmony and his desire that they should all be friends and love each other. The queen says that Clarence should be included in this celebration of unity and harmony: Richard pretends to be shocked and outraged, and tells them that Clarence is dead, which they hadn't known. The king is shocked because he had ordered Clarence to be freed from the Tower, but Richard tells him that this second order arrived too late to save him.

3.2 Summaries

King Edward is deeply saddened by the news of Clarence's death. He exits with the queen. Speaking to the remaining nobles, Richard suggests that the queen and her followers are responsible for the death of Clarence.

Richard accuses the queen of Clarence's death

Act II Scene 2
In the palace, the Duchess of York and Clarence's two children enter. The children want to know if their father is dead, which the duchess denies. But the children have heard a lot to make them think he has been killed. The boy says the king is to blame for his father's death and his sister agrees. The duchess tells them the king is not to blame, but the boy tells her that Richard had told him that the queen had pushed the king into executing Clarence. The duchess is shocked and says that Richard is a traitor and that she is ashamed of his deceitful and devious nature.

Queen Elizabeth enters with a couple of nobles, Rivers and Dorset. She is loudly mourning her husband's death. The children challenge Elizabeth's grief, claiming theirs is greater: The duchess claims that her grief is greater than anyone else's.

Kind Edward is dead

Richard and other nobles enter. They all discuss putting the young prince on the throne.

The others leave, and Richard and Buckingham remain. Buckingham refers to a secret plot, which remains unclear.

Act II Scene 3
Three citizens on the streets of London discuss the situation in the country following King Edward's death. The citizens are frightened of the prospect of Richard taking power, and are also wary of the queen's relatives.

3.2 Summaries

Act II Scene 4
In the palace in London, Queen Elizabeth, the Duchess of York, the Archbishop of York and the young Duke of York meet. The duchess and duke make fun of Richard. A messenger comes in to tell them that some of Elizabeth's followers have been imprisoned by Richard and Buckingham.

Act III
Act III Scene 1
On a London street, Prince Edward is greeted by Richard, Buckingham and others as he enters the city. The mayor arrives, followed by Hastings. Hastings tells the prince that his mother and the young Duke of York have taken sanctuary somewhere else. Buckingham sends the cardinal and Hastings to get the young duke.

Edward, Richard and Buckingham talk about the Tower of London, about fame and history and posterity.

Hastings and the cardinal return with the young Duke of York. The duke and Edward make fun of Richard. Richard says the two young nobles should go to the Tower, which they reluctantly do.

Richard makes plans

All exit but Richard, Buckingham and Catesby. They complain about the Duke of York's wit and insolence towards Richard, saying he has been encouraged in this direction by his mother the duchess. The three nobles then discuss Richard's plot, and Catesby is sent to Hastings to find out whether he will join them or not.

Richard promises Buckingham that he will be richly rewarded when he is king.

Act III Scene 2
A messenger to Hastings from the Earl of Derby tells Hastings that Derby has dreamed a dark omen of the danger Richard poses to

both of them. The messenger tells Hastings that Derby suggests they both flee to the north to get away from Richard. Hastings dismisses Derby's fears, saying that there's nothing to worry about. He sends the messenger back to Derby with a message to accompany him to the Tower later.

Catesby enters. They talk about the insecure state of the country, and when Catesby says that only Richard becoming king will settle the chaos, Hastings mocks him and says that he would not support Richard for the throne.

> Insecure state of the country

Stanley, Earl of Derby appears. Hastings and Derby head off for the Tower.

Hastings talks with a couple of people on the way and then is met by Buckingham, who talks in asides about how Hastings is heading to his death.

Act III Scene 3
In Yorkshire, Rivers, Grey and Vaughan are being led to their deaths by execution. The nobles talk, recalling Queen Margaret's curse (Act I Scene 3).

> Rivers, Grey and Vaughan are executed

Act III Scene 4
The Tower of London: Buckingham, Hastings, Derby and other nobles are gathered to discuss the coronation. Richard comes in briefly and tells Buckingham that Hastings is not to be trusted and should be executed. He then leaves.

Richard soon returns with Buckingham and accuses Hastings of being a traitor, and accuses Queen Elizabeth of having used witchcraft on him. He orders Hastings to be executed.

> Richard accuses Hastings

Hastings recalls Margaret's curse.

3.2 Summaries

Act III Scene 5
Inside the Tower of London: Richard and Buckingham are preparing to fake deep grief and worry about the state of the realm. They put on a show of panic and alarm when the Lord Mayor enters. When Hastings' severed head is brought in, Richard pretends to be sorry for his death.

Buckingham persuades the mayor to explain to the general public why it was right to have Hastings executed.

Richard tells Buckingham to spread rumours about Edward's character and illegitimacy.

Act III Scene 6
A scrivener complains about the injustice done to Hastings.

Act III Scene 7
Buckingham reports to Richard on his success in praising Richard and slandering Edward (and his children) to the London citizens. He says that most of the people were more suspicious than supportive.

Richard and Buckingham plan to put on a show of Richard's piety and pretend that he is unwilling to take power, thereby forcing the mayor and others to persuade him to take the throne.

Richard leaves the stage and the mayor enters, accompanied by citizens. Buckingham makes a show of sending Catesby off to find Richard and plays up Richard's faked devotion and prayers.

Richard returns, flanked by two bishops. Buckingham and Richard enter into a lengthy and complex discussion, hypocritical and exaggerated, designed to make a display of Richard's moral, modest reluctance to accept the crown and Buckingham's impassioned demands that he acknowledge his "right" and the love of the English people.

3.2 Summaries

The mayor and Catesby join Buckingham in persuading Richard to become king. Eventually, Richard gives in to their pleas and agrees to take the throne.

Richard agrees to take the throne

Act IV
Act IV Scene 1
Queen Elizabeth and Anne, the Duchess of Gloucester (now married to Richard) are heading to the Tower to visit the young princes. Other noblewomen are with them. Brakenbury stops them from entering, saying it is on Richard's orders (Richard is currently the Lord Protector: he has not yet been crowned king).

Derby enters and tells Anne to come with him to Richard's coronation.

Act IV Scene 2
The palace in London: Richard, now King Richard III, enters with Buckingham, Catesby and others. He tells Buckingham that he wants the young princes killed, because he feels they represent a threat to his position. Buckingham seems to be shocked at the order to have the princes murdered, and asks for some time to think about it.

Richard sends a page to fetch Tyrell, a potential killer for hire.

Richard says in an aside that he now doubts Buckingham's loyalty.

Stanley, Earl of Derby, enters and tells Richard that Dorset has fled to Richmond. Richard orders Stanley to spread a rumour that Anne is very ill and dying. Richard plans to get rid of Anne and marry his niece, after killing her brothers. He sees this as being the only way to solidify and strengthen his position on the throne.

Richard wants to kill Anne and the young princes

Tyrell enters and receives his orders from Richard – to go to the Tower and kill the young princes.

3.2 Summaries

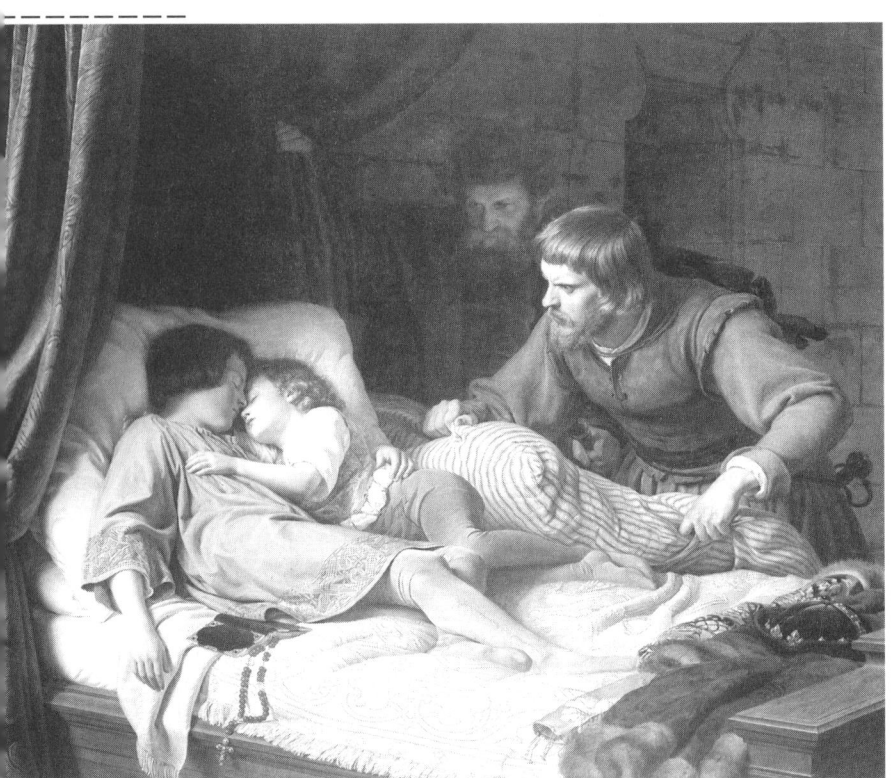

The Murder of the Children of King Edward: painted in 1835 by Theodor Hildebrandt.
© picture alliance/akg-images

Buckingham returns. He tries to get Richard's attention and the king's word that what he had been promised will be given to him, but Richard ignores him. He calls repeatedly but Richard pretends not to hear. When he finally does order Buckingham to state his wishes, he refuses him and appears to be cold and hostile towards him.

Left alone on the stage, Buckingham says he will flee London, because he is now sure that he is in danger from Richard's evil plans.

Buckingham is afraid of Richard

Act IV Scene 3
The palace: Tyrell enters and says that the princes have been killed. The two men he had carry out the murders struggled with their consciences when they saw the young children, but they killed them, and now Tyrell has come to give King Richard the news.

Richard promises to reward him. Tyrell leaves and Richard summarises the current state of affairs: his brother Clarence's children are dealt with, Edward's sons are dead, his wife Anne is dead, and now he believes Richmond is looking to marry Richard's niece Elizabeth, to strengthen his own claim to the throne.

Ratcliff enters and tells Richard that Buckingham is forming an army with Welsh support and Morton has joined Richmond.

Richard prepares for war.

Act IV Scene 4
Old Queen Margaret is outside the palace, enjoying her enemies' sufferings and pains. The Duchess of York and Queen Elizabeth enter.

The three women voice their grief at the deaths in their families. Margaret accuses the duchess (Richard's mother) of having given birth to a "hell hound" that is seeking to destroy them all. Margaret curses Richard, and Elizabeth asks her to teach her how to curse properly.

Margaret leaves and Richard enters. The duchess and Elizabeth begin cursing him, and he demands that trumpeters play to drown out the voices of the women. He argues with the duchess, who curses him again and then exits.

3.2 Summaries

Richard plans to marry his niece Elizabeth

Richard and Elizabeth talk and he tells her that he wants to marry her daughter (also called Elizabeth). Elizabeth is horrified by the idea, not only because Richard has killed her sons (the younger Elizabeth's brothers), but also because of the incestuous nature of the relationship, Richard being her uncle.

Richard uses all of his rhetorical skill and overwhelming oratory to persuade her to push her daughter into the marriage.

She exits and Ratcliff and Catesby enter. They bring reports of a navy massing to the West, apparently under the command of Richmond. Messengers enter with news of rebellion across the country, also that Buckingham's army has been broken up and Buckingham has been taken prisoner.

Richard orders various nobles to meet him at Salisbury, and demands that the captive Buckingham should also be brought there.

Act IV Scene 5
At Derby's house, Stanley (Derby) talks with another noble, Sir Christopher Urswick. Derby tells him that his son is being held hostage. Urswick reports that many more nobles are joining Richmond's rebellious forces.

Act V
Act V Scene 1
At Salisbury: Buckingham is being led to his execution. He talks about his guilt, and remembers Margaret's curse from the beginning.

Act V Scene 2
Richmond's camp: he and other nobles discuss their military plans, and are confident that many of Richard's supporters will change sides as soon as they can.

3.2 Summaries

Act V Scene 3
At Bosworth Field, Richard and Richmond are preparing for the battle. Richard seems quite nervous and restless. Richmond prays to God for success in the battle to come.

That night, both Richmond and Richard are haunted by ghosts – **the ghosts of the people Richard has had killed**. The ghosts support Richmond and bless him, but they curse Richard and wish for his death.

Visit from the ghosts

Afterwards, Richard is even more anxious and chaotic, babbling away in hectic demands and arguments with himself. Richmond delivers a stirring **motivational speech to his followers** as they head off for the battle.

Richard enters with some of his nobles. They discuss Richmond's potential weakness in military matters, and they talk about their strategies for the coming battle. Richard then gives a speech to his army. Whereas Richmond's speech was a positive and rousing one, Richard's is full of spite, insults, venom and anger. He paints a threatening and fearful picture of how evil Richmond and his followers are.

Act V Scene 4
In the battle. Richard's horse has been killed and he calls for a new one: "A horse! a horse! my kingdom for a horse!" (ll. 8. 13) He has killed many men and now desperately wants to find and kill Richmond.

Richmond kills Richard in battle. He takes the crown and says he will marry Elizabeth, the daughter of King Edward IV. He declares the devastating and ruinous civil wars – the *Wars of the Roses* – to be finally finished.

Richard is killed by Richmond

3.3 Structure

SUMMARY

> Shakespeare's *Richard III* is a classic tragedy with a five-act structure.

Shakespeare and his contemporaries generally organised their plays in five acts. It was only from the 18th century onwards that the three-act structure became more popular and more widely used.

In the 19th century, the German writer **Gustav Freytag** (1816–1895) developed an important analysis of the five-act structure in dramas. According to Freytag, the five acts have the following functions:

→ **Exposition (or Introduction)**
The setting is introduced: the place, the time and the characters. The exposition can also contain elements of the "backstory" – what has happened to our characters before the opening of the play?

→ **Rising action**
This is what sets the plot – the engine of the story – in motion. The rising action refers to those events which set the characters on their dramatic courses, whether of collision or cooperation.

→ **Climax**
This is not the end of the story: it is the point at which the protagonist's course or journey becomes changed by the engine of the plot (peripeteia). From this point on, the protagonist is revealed in all their strength or weakness as they face their fate and the consequences of the rising action from Act II.

→ **Falling action**
The protagonist faces the hostility of the opposing forces – opposed characters and dangerous events.
→ **Catastrophe or resolution / revelation**
The protagonist faces the logical, unavoidable conclusion of his or her dramatic arc.

This structure for the classic (Aristotelian) drama is called **Freytag's pyramid**, because when the dramatic structure is expressed in visual terms, it looks like this:

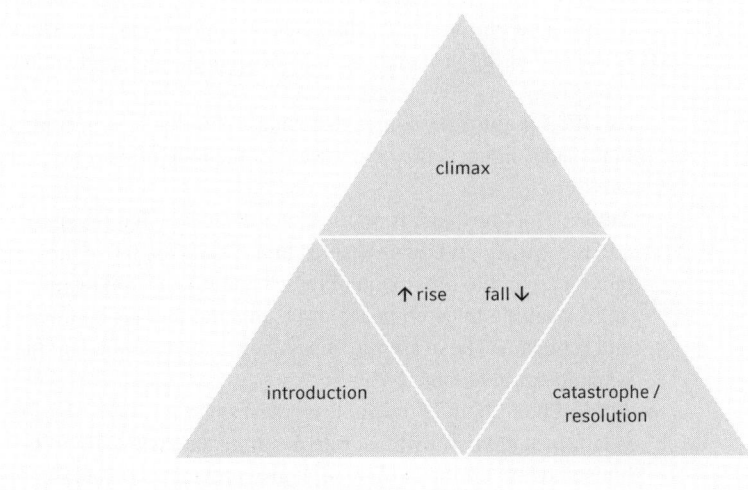

This structure **describes a dramatic arc** that is generally followed by most forms of storytelling – a story grows and rises towards a

3.3 Structure

crisis, from which it moves towards the resolution. With a stage play, however, the structure is more visible to the audience than it would be to a person reading a novel or watching a film – the changing of scenes and the movement of characters is more exposed on stage than it is in other storytelling forms.

So how does *Richard III* conform to this structure? Almost exactly, as we can see if we sketch the broad strokes of the play's events:

→ **Act I:** We have a first act in which the scene is set (place and time) and the characters are introduced, most importantly Richard – the protagonist. We are also given sketches of the backstory.

→ **Act II:** During the second act, Richard and his followers commit murder and plot to destroy his enemies and gain power. This is the rise of the protagonist; he is driving the plot, and acting proactively.

→ **Act III:** The third act comes to a climax with Richard becoming king. This climax is the goal towards which the protagonist was working.

→ **Act IV:** The fourth act is about Richard's increasing paranoia and the growing rebellion against him. This is the fall of the protagonist – on the other side of the climax (the accomplishment of his goal) he finds no peace or victory, but increasing anxiety and rebellion. These are the consequences of his actions; this is his inexorable fate.

→ **Act V:** The fifth and final act is a catastrophe for Richard, the villain-protagonist, with his rule destroyed in civil war and he himself dying on the battlefield. It also provides a resolution for the country, with the civil wars finally ending and peace being restored.

3.4 Characters

> **SUMMARY**
>
> The characters of *Richard III* are broadly grouped in their belonging to, or being allied with, one of the two great dynasties of the country: Lancaster or York.

Possibly the single biggest obstacle to getting to grips with *Richard III*, after **the difficulty of the language**, is the cast of characters. There are lots of them: they are often called by different names (Richard, Gloucester, Duke of Gloucester, et cetera); and many of them have the same name (there are at least three Edwards in the play, for example[6]). To make things even more complicated, **the characters are grouped in different factions** which also change allegiance and identity during the play. Luckily, some of the named characters do not require our full attention, as they mostly serve as messengers or sources of information, and are not fully rounded characters with any real impact on the plot or Richard's career. Ratcliff and Lovell are two examples of this kind of "functional" character, from whom we learn things as if from a bulletin.

And there is yet another interesting complication: this is a play in which **the main character tells lies all the time**. Richard almost never tells the truth, except in the asides to the audience in the earlier scenes. He constantly deceives those around him, whether they are allies or enemies, and twists the truth to cast suspicion on other characters for his own evil deeds.

Large number of names in the play

---

[6] King Edward IV, his son Edward (young Prince of Wales) and Edward of Westminster (Lady Anne's intended husband).

3.4 Characters

Language

As with so many aspects of this play, and indeed any Shakespearean drama, **the best advice is to not expect that you will understand everything the first time you read it**. The language is difficult and confusing; the action is often described or conducted indirectly; and there are far too many characters for anyone to be able to understand everything in one sitting. You will have to get used to re-reading passages to get at the content. **Studying Shakespeare is hard work, but it's worthwhile**: the black comedy of *Richard III* and the evil, cynical plotting of the main character are fascinating and entertaining enough to be a reward for the effort it will take you to understand this complex and lengthy play.

Main characters – House of York
Richard, later King Richard III

Protagonist of the play

First appears: Act I, Scene 1. Richard is the **Duke of Gloucester**. He has two brothers, King Edward IV and George, Duke of Clarence. **Their mother is the Duchess of York**. Richard is the youngest of the three brothers.

Richard is the protagonist of the play – **he is the central character**, and the structure of the drama follows his actions and their consequences. But he is not a hero: he is a cynical and deceitful man who intentionally **performs evil acts to increase his own power**. Richard even introduces himself at the beginning of the play as a villain (I.1.30). He feels excluded from the joys and pleasures of peace time by his **physical deformities** and ambitious, restless nature. He plots to play his brothers off against one another for his own benefit.

Evil intentions

As he describes himself, he is deformed, hideous enough to make dogs bark (I.1.23). His physical ugliness is the expression of the vicious and unnatural nature of his soul and personality. Everything about Richard, he tells us himself in his opening speech, is somehow

3.4 Characters

wrong: "Cheated of feature by dissembling nature" (I.1.19), he is unnatural both in his ambition and evil intentions, aiming to harm his own brothers, and in his physical form.

The play follows Richard's wicked **plans to manipulate, murder and deceive his way to the throne**, to become King of England. We see him lying, manipulating and pretending in different circumstances to make people around him do what he wants. But gaining the throne doesn't calm him down at all: his restless and deceitful nature turns on those around him, and he becomes increasingly paranoid when faced with the growing rebellion of Buckingham and other nobles, and he continues to be haunted by the idea that other natural heirs to the throne – the young princes locked in the tower – may pose a threat to him and his rule.

Richard is driven and motivated by ambition, but as he makes clear in his opening speech, there are other, uglier forces driving him: his resentment and hatred of others more blessed than he is, in his view – his ugliness and deformity of body and soul become for him **a self-fulfilling prophecy**. It is as if he sets out intentionally to make his life and deeds as ugly and unnatural as his twisted body.

But the remarkable thing about the character of Richard is the way in which he binds us, the audience, to his character and course. The play begins with him **addressing us directly**, telling us in brutal and entertaining honesty how he has decided to embrace evil and use his wits to take what has been denied him by birth. This candour, and the irresistible force of his rhetoric and arguments, make him **a complex figure** with whom we may not exactly sympathise, but in whom we are interested and whom we are more than willing to follow in his career of evil. One of the last times we see Richard unleash his gift for **deceptive and seductive rhetoric** is in the climactic Act III Scene 6, in which he and Buckingham put on a dazzlingly hypocritical show of modesty and piety in order to trick

Margin notes:
- complex, ambiguous and highly changeable relationship with the main character
- Lady Anne despite explicit knowledge of his wickedness allow themselves to be seduced
- charismatic/fascinating — be impressed with him by his brilliant wordplay
- Aim: Becoming King of England
- his skillful argumentation and his relentless pursuit of his selfish desires
- Opening speech to the audience

3.4 Characters

the Lord Mayor of London, and the citizens of London, to demand that Richard take the throne to save the country from all of these terrible dangers (specifically: Richard's opponents).

Division between us and the protagonist

But this also changes as the play progresses. As he becomes increasingly **isolated from the other characters in the play**, as they either die (are murdered) or turn against him, so too does the figure of Richard lose his connection with us, the audience. The asides (a figure on stage addressing the audience rather than other characters within the play) become less frequent after Act I. By the later stages of the play he is hardly ever addressing the audience, and his entertaining and inexorable rhetoric has been replaced by **brief and blunt demands for information**. Almost all of the characters left alive have turned against him, and Shakespeare has also managed to force a division between us and the protagonist.

This decay of Richard's character is first seen in his growing paranoia (see III.4.58–61). The moral lesson in his decay is that **an evil and corrupt nature will only see evil and corruption around it**; as well as forcing political chaos by his actions, he is stirring the chaos within himself by staining everything around him with **terror and blood**. He blames his own physical deformities on the "witchcraft" of two women (III.4.66–71). All it takes is for Hastings to question "if" this is actually what has happened – and Richard immediately sentences him to death.

Paranoia

His paranoia only increases once he has taken the throne (which happens officially at the beginning of Act IV Scene 2). His order to Buckingham that the young princes should be executed is blatant and brutal, and when Buckingham doesn't immediately respond to support this plan to murder children, **Richard begins to suspect him**, too – his most loyal and effective ally among the nobles.

By the eve of the final battle (Act V Scene 4) Richard is hardly recognisable. He repeatedly asks the same question (asking for pen

3.4 Characters

and paper) and appears lost in insignificant details and paralyzed by paranoia.

When **the ghosts appear** to both Richmond and Richard, Richard hears an intense stream of curses and vengeance, with the ghosts all demanding that he "despair and die".

"despair and die"

Another split screen contrast is in the way **the two leaders address their armies**: Richmond (V.3.239–271) urges faith, hope and love; Richard (V.3.315–338) rambles incoherently about how weak and pathetic their enemies are, about how they will rape his followers' daughters, and throws insults around at everyone.

Richard fights bravely and wildly during the battle, but he is eventually **confronted by Richmond** and dies in combat. Richmond's final speech, closing the play (V.4.28–55) is striking in how swiftly and completely it moves past Richard into the hopeful, peaceful future: the wicked, deformed wretch who has dominated the fate of his country and caused such trouble and grief **is blown away in defeat**, vanishing into history. His evil career left him with literally nothing, swept away even in death.

Richard dies

King Edward IV

At the opening of the play, Edward is sick and dying (Queen Elizabeth and her nobles discuss the king's poor health at the beginning of Act I Scene 3).

The king appears on stage at the opening of Act II, in the palace, surrounded by nobles from **the two enemy factions** – those gathered around Queen Elizabeth, and those loyal to Richard. Edward is very ill and knows he is dying. When we first see him on stage, he is attempting to persuade the mutually hostile factions in the palace **to make peace with one another**.

The current King of England, elder brother to Richard and George (Clarence)

Edward dies offstage, and his death and the consequences thereof are discussed by three citizens in the short scene III.3.

3.4 Characters

George, Duke of Clarence

The next in line to the throne after King Edward IV

Clarence first appears in Act I Scene 1. He is being taken to the Tower of London under guard. The king believes false rumours spread by Richard which implicate Clarence in a plot to murder the king's children. Richard's aim in framing Clarence is to remove another obstacle between him, Richard, and the throne of England.

Clarence is gullible and innocent. He confesses his guilty feelings and fears of death to a guard at the Tower. Later, he is murdered by assassins (one refuses at the end to kill him, but the other murderer finishes the job) and learns from them that he has been **betrayed by Richard**, who has sent the killers.

Duchess of York

Mother of the three brothers

We meet the Duchess of York, mother to Edward, Richard and Clarence, in Act II Scene 2. She is attempting to calm Clarence's children, who have heard that he has been murdered.

The Duchess of York feels that **she has suffered more than any other individual**, and even argues with Queen Elizabeth about who has the greater grief and who has suffered more (II.2 – this scene acquires an even more blackly comical tone once the two orphaned children of Clarence join in the chorus of competitive grief).

Confronted with Richard after he has taken the crown, (IV.4.137+) she tells him that **she wishes she had killed him** in the womb.

Queen Elizabeth

Wife of King Edward IV

Also known as **Lady Grey**, she is the wife of King Edward IV. She first enters the stage in Act I Scene 3, accompanied by nobles loyal to her, Lord Rivers and Lord Grey. She is worried about the king's poor health, and **fears for what will happen** to her and their son Prince Edward once he dies. She knows that Richard, who has been named Protector of the Prince, is neither her ally nor her friend.

3.4 Characters

→ he knows she poses a real threat

Early in the play, Richard spends a lot of time and effort stirring up hatred and suspicion of Elizabeth.

The young Prince Edward
This young prince appears onstage in III.1. He is being welcomed into London by Richard and Buckingham. It immediately becomes clear that **this boy is extremely intelligent and observant**, and that he understands that devious plotting has led to his natural allies being absent, and his mother and brother have fled to take sanctuary in a secret place.

Edward IV & Elizabeth's son

Edward clearly distrusts Richard, and when Richard suggests that he should go to the Tower for his own safety until his coronation, Edward is suspicious.

Richard is displeased to find the boy so clever and sharp, but he manages to have both this young prince and the young Duke of York **sent to the Tower**, allegedly for their own protection.

Murdered by Richard

The young Duke of York
This child (young prince Richard) first appears in II.4, where he indulges in some mockery of his uncle Richard's nature and appearance. When he and the young Prince Edward meet (III.1.96–150) the difference is remarkable in intelligence, wit and maturity between the young Duke – with a child's rhetoric and humour – and Edward, a clever, quick-witted and educated mind. But despite their arguments and taunts, the two young nobles, **threats to Richard's ambition for the throne**, are sent for their own protection – allegedly – to the Tower of London.

Edward IV & Elizabeth's son, brother to young Prince Edward

Boy and Girl
These two children are just pieces in the game the adults are playing: the Duchess of York tries to hide the death of their father Clarence

Clarence's children

3.4 Characters

from them, but they see immediately that she is lying; Richard has been lying to them about what happened, teaching them that the queen is to blame for their father's murder (II.2.20–26).

The Woodvilles
→ Queen Elizabeth's sons from her first marriage and her brother.

Marquess of Dorset

Son of Queen Elizabeth

Dorset flees to Richmond and survives.

Lord Grey

Son of Queen Elizabeth

Following King Edward's death, he is imprisoned by Richard and Buckingham with other York loyalists.

Earl Rivers

Queen Elizabeth's brother

Rivers (Anthony Woodville) was involved in the imprisonment of Hastings (before the play begins). We learn in III.3 that he has been imprisoned by Richard and Buckingham, along with other supporters of the House of York, following the death of King Edward.

Women of the House of Lancaster
Old Queen Margaret
Margaret is an old woman, widow of King Henry VI and mother to Edward. **She and Richard hate one another:** Lady Anne talks about an incident where Richard tried to stab Margaret and had to be restrained by his brothers (I.2.95–98). She appears on stage in Act I Scene 3, entering quietly while Richard and Queen Elizabeth are fighting. She knows Richard killed her husband, Henry, and her son, Edward: she calls Richard a devil.

Margaret curses Richard

Margaret is an important figure in the play because of the curses she speaks in Act I Scene 3. She is old, alone, exiled on pain

3.4 Characters

[Handwritten margin note at top: "impotent, overpowering rage she directs at Richard and his family stands for the helpless, righteous anger of all of Richard's victims | without a husband to grant her status and security, she is reduced to depending on the charity of her family's murderers to survive"]

of death, but chooses to remain in London to curse Richard. Her curse is that he should live long enough to see the loss of all he holds dear. She curses him with paranoia and distrust, attacks of conscience and spiritual restlessness and turmoil.

Margaret is old enough and isolated enough to have **no more fear of anyone or anything**. She freely curses all who have contributed to the losses she has suffered, and specifically curses all those who have allied themselves with Richard or enabled his grasp for greater power. Her curses are powerful in tone and effect: in the chapter in this study guide on Themes in the play (p. 61), we will look more deeply into the hints of the supernatural throughout *Richard III*, including Margaret's fearsome curses.

She advises Buckingham, whom she knows to be innocent of the crimes against her family, to be careful with Richard, warning the nobleman that Richard is a dangerous and untrustworthy monster.

Warns Buckingham

She reappears later (IV.4) to enjoy the miseries and failures of her enemies.

Lady Anne

Widow of Edward, Prince of Wales, who was the son of King Henry VI: later Richard's wife. We first see Anne in the second scene of the first act. She is in mourning, accompanying the body of King Henry VI. Richard has killed both Henry and her intended husband Edward.

Daughter-in-law of King Henry VI

Anne hates Richard and curses him. The first time we see them meet she is furious with him, but gradually gives in to his persuasive, deceitful rhetoric. It is difficult to follow quite why she begins to soften towards this evil man who has confessed to the murders: he overwhelms her with flattery and false emotions, and she warily accepts a ring from him and **agrees to meet him elsewhere once the old king has been buried**. Richard also shows some surprise at

3.4 Characters

how easy it was for him to overcome her grief. He feels contempt for her, and it is hard for the audience to not also feel that this grieving woman has maybe given in to flattery a little too quickly, showing her to be a shallow person with more vanity than sense.

Anne comments on exactly this (IV.1.77–86) when she and other noblewomen are refused entry to the Tower to visit in the captive young princes. She acknowledges that her "woman's heart / Grossly grew captive to his honey words".

Richard murders Anne to marry his niece

Richard only understands other people as tools to be used for his goals or as obstacles to be removed as brutally as possible. **Anne, now his wife, is a tool he no longer needs** (Act IV Scene 2): she has served her purpose and is now an obstacle. He intends to marry his niece, and in preparation for this, he orders Stanley and Catesby to spread rumours that Anne is deathly ill (IV.2.51). In doing this he prepares the ground for her murder, freeing him to marry his niece and further solidify his grip on the throne.

Other nobles
Earl of Richmond (Henry Tudor)

Later King Henry VII: Derby's stepson

Richmond (House of Tudor) becomes the focal point of the **rebellion against Richard's mad and evil rule**. As the play progresses more and more nobles go to join him, including many of the noblewomen. Richard recalls prophecies (Act IV Scene 2) about Richmond which frighten him, driving him deeper into his paranoia. He also fears that Richmond may seek to marry Elizabeth, Richard's niece, to secure a claim to the throne.

The rebellion against Richard grows in the distance during Act IV, with Richard hearing from different sources how Richmond has taken to the seas to come to England from France. More and more noble houses pledge their allegiance to Richmond. In Act V Scene 2 we enter Richmond's rebel camp for the first time. He has gathered

3.4 Characters

with many nobles loyal to him and opposed to the rule of Richard – **Oxford, Blunt, Herbert and others**.

Richmond articulates the contempt and hatred of Richard felt by all who oppose him: he talks of him in terms of the "boar", the "foul swine", referencing Richard's heraldic beast, the boar. Richmond and his allies are sure that Richard's supporters will swiftly change sides if given the opportunity – they are convinced that there is no love or loyalty in their allegiance to the wicked King Richard, and that most would rather come back to the side of peace and good.

Richmond's speeches and those of his followers are easy to contrast with Richard's: they are concerned with restoring peace and order, whereas Richard's career has been dominated by ambition and evil. An even more explicit contrast comes in Act V Scene 3, when both Richmond and Richard are **visited at night by ghosts of Richard's victims**. These ghosts promise support and encouragement for Richmond while cursing and harassing Richard. These supernatural visitations are the most explicit literary device Shakespeare uses to highlight **the morality of power** and the consequences of abusing power.

Opponent to Richard

> An **American saying** popular with Christians is "character is who you are when no one is looking", meaning that when you are alone (with God) and no longer playing a role or putting up a facade for others, you are at your realest. This idea can be applied to the encounters with the ghosts on the eve of the battle. When characters in a play are alone on stage and talking so that only we, the audience, can hear, then we can always assume that this is the realest self finding expression. Bearing

3.4 Characters

> this in mind, compare and contrast Richmond's speech before sleeping (V.3.109–118) with any of Richard's incoherent, hate-filled ramblings in this final act.

Richmond addresses the gathered rebels on the morning of the final battle, reminding them that God is on their side, and that Richard is "a bloody tyrant and a homicide" (V.3.247). He is passionately **convinced of the moral rightness** of what he is leading them to do: his speech inspires love and hope for a better time to come.

Justice and fairness

And at the end of the play, in his final speech, **Richmond promises to reunite the major dynasties**, to bring peace to the country after such a long time of civil wars and unrest: he sees a future of peaceful happiness and success now that the conflicts are ended.

Shakespeare's intention

In writing the character this way, as such a strong symbol of the rightness of moral royal power, Shakespeare was showing his allegiance to the contemporary powers in his own place and time: **the royal house of Tudor**.

Lord Hastings

The Lord Chamberlain

First appearing in the opening scene, Hastings has just been released from imprisonment in the Tower. He had been imprisoned under orders from the queen and her brother Lord Rivers (Anthony Woodville).

When Richard's plotting begins in earnest, he sends his loyal ally Catesby to find out whether Hastings will be on his side in the struggles to come. Hastings is evidently not interested: **he speaks of Richard with contempt**. Buckingham suggests indirectly that he will pay with his life for his lack of loyalty to Richard.

3.4 Characters

Hastings tragically misunderstands and underestimates Richard's nature, his murderous ambition and complete lack of all scruples. He laughs at the prospect of Richard wearing the crown (III.2), and promises that a year from now they will all be laughing at the idea. This unfortunate failure of understanding on his part is typical for a character who is not particularly intelligent, and worse, is easily persuaded and convinced by smooth rhetoric. Repeatedly throughout the play, **we see Hastings blatantly misunderstanding the danger he is in**. When Buckingham coaxes him into believing that he is one of Richard's favourites (III.4), even though we have seen Hastings publicly mock Richard, Hastings still believes him.

He underestimates the danger

Hastings is sentenced to death by Richard in III.4. The final straw, for Richard, comes when Hastings asks "if" Richard's deformed arm is the result of "witchcraft" perpetrated by Queen Elizabeth. Finally, and far too late, Hastings understands how evil and devious Richard has been, and **how blind he has been to the chaos Richard is stoking.** He also recalls old Queen Margaret's curse, seeing how right she was in damning Richard and all who follow him, and acknowledging the old queen's foresightedness in grasping how much damage Richard's evil ambition will inflict on those around him and on the country as a whole.

Old Queen Margaret's curse

Lord Stanley

A noble first seen being loyal to Richard, appearing at the beginning of Act I Scene 3. By III.2 however he has come to suspect how dangerous Richard has become, and sends a messenger to Hastings to warn him. Hastings unwisely rejects Stanley's warnings.

Earl of Derby; stepfather of Richmond

3.4 Characters

Supporters of Richard
Duke of Buckingham
Buckingham first appears at the opening of Act I Scene 3. **He is allied with Richard**, and tries to persuade Queen Elizabeth and her followers to make peace with Richard and his faction. He is deeply involved with Richard's plotting: he advises Richard on how to test the loyalty of individual noblemen (see for example III.1). At this relatively early stage of Richard's ascension to the throne, **Buckingham is an intelligent and loyal advisor**. In return for his loyalty, Richard promises to reward Buckingham with the title Earl of Hereford.

Richard's henchman

Buckingham assists Richard in his plotting and deceit. We see him taking instructions on how **to fake an emotional reaction** in order to deceive the Lord Mayor of London (opening of III.5), and we often see him supporting Richard's plots with a full understanding of how deceitfully and wickedly the Duke of Gloucester is behaving.

He is loyal and effective, and so it comes as a surprise to us, the audience, and to Buckingham too, when Richard suddenly and irrationally turns on him in Act IV Scene 2. He suspects Buckingham of being disloyal because he is not equally eager to murder the young princes in the Tower. Richard says Buckingham will no longer "be the neighbour to my counsel" (IV.2.43).

Buckingham has been close enough to Richard to be able to tell when his luck runs out (IV.2.118–121), and with the example of Hastings' sudden death before him, **he flees the city to save his own life**.

In the end, he's Richard's opponent

As Richmond's rebellion gathers numbers and strength, Buckingham also summons troops, from Wales, to join the uprising against Richard. But as reported in IV.4.508–514, Buckingham's forces are caught in a flood and scattered, and Buckingham himself has vanished. Soon after, Richard learns that Buckingham has

3.4 Characters

been captured, and he orders him to be brought to the town of Salisbury.

> **Act V Scene 1**
> Buckingham has been captured following the disastrous end to his armed uprising against Richard. He is being led to his execution.
> This is the single most important scene for understanding Buckingham's character and role in the play. He sees that he has been instrumental in carrying out Richard's "underhand corrupted foul injustice" (V.1.6), and that he must face his death for the crimes he has committed and abetted. Importantly, he also mentions Margaret and her powerful curses.

Sir Richard Ratcliff
Richard's supporter and executioner.

Sir William Catesby
Catesby is a **loyal ally of Richard**, and performs many tasks for him. He is sent to Hastings to test his loyalty to Richard, and is involved enough in Richard murderous ambitions to understand that the wrong answers will send Hastings to his death. At Richard's orders, he spreads rumours that his wife Anne is deathly ill, in preparation for Richard having her murdered.

Lord Lovel
One of Richard's supporters, who takes Lord Hastings to his execution.

3.4 Characters

Sir Robert Brakenbury

Lieutenant of the Tower

First appearing in Act I Scene 1, we see Brakenbury escorting Richard's younger brother Clarence to be imprisoned in the Tower of London at the command of the king. Later we see him again carrying out Richard's orders: in Act IV Scene 1 Brakenbury stops the Duchess of York, Queen Elizabeth and Lady Anne (by now married to Richard) from entering the Tower of London to see the young princes Richard has had imprisoned there. He makes a slip of the tongue, referring to Richard as "King" while he is still officially only Lord Protector (IV.1.17–19), which tells us a lot about his sense of **allegiance to the murderous Richard**.

Earl of Surrey
One of Richard's supporters.

Duke of Norfolk
Richard's supporter in the Battle of Bosworth.

Further characters
Archbishop of York
The Archbishop first appears in III.4 following the death of King Edward. He is close to the Duchess of York and Queen Elizabeth, warning them to flee and hide from the danger posed by Richard.

Lord Cardinal, Archbishop of Canterbury

Bishop of Ely

Priests
→ Sir Christopher Urswick
→ Sir John

3.4 Characters

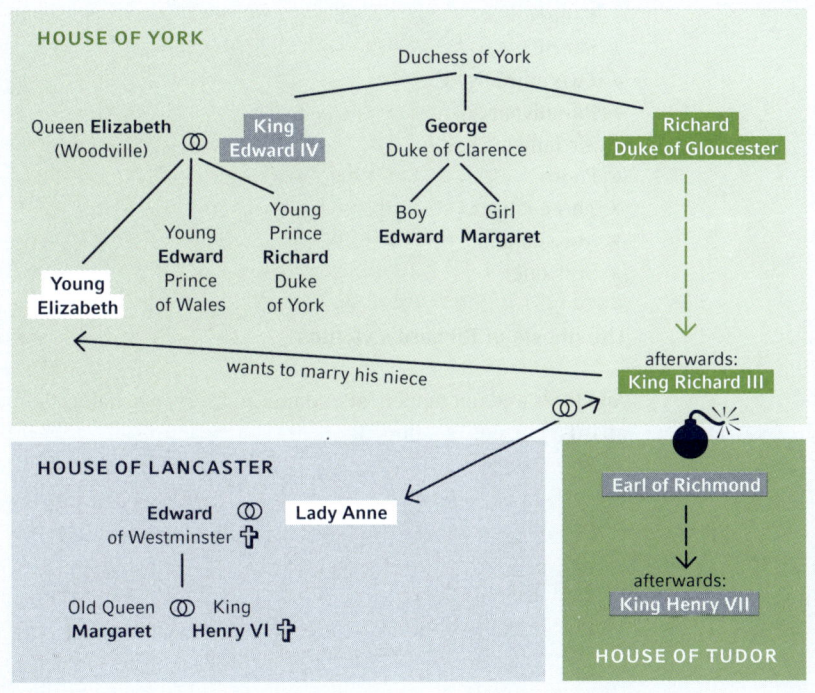

Lord mayor of London

The Mayor is thoroughly deceived by Richard and Buckingham in Act III Scene 5. They have orchestrated their deceits and lies to make him believe that Hastings had been a dangerous traitor, and later, they trick him into pleading that Richard should take power to save the country from chaos.

3.4 Characters

Citizens and commoners
- → Keeper
- → Sheriff
- → Two murderers
- → Pursuivant
- → Sir James Tyrrell
- → Page
- → Three citizens
- → Messengers
- → Scrivener

The ghosts of Richard's victims

And lords and gentlemen, attendants and servants, halberdiers and guards, citizens, soldiers ...

3.5 Notes on themes

> Because so many of the themes in Shakespeare's history play *Richard III* are so densely interconnected, we look at them in three groups:
> → Morality
> → Ambition & power
> → Fate & free will.

SUMMARY

The history plays: genre and themes

In writing his history plays, using figures and events drawn **from chronicles of English history**, Shakespeare could rely on his audiences being fully familiar with the subject matter. Five hundred years later, we have to research who did what, where and when and why – but the dynastic struggles of the *Wars of the Roses* and **the conflicts between major noble families** were as well-known to contemporary audiences as, for example, the broad facts of the First and Second World Wars and the (historically) brief history of the GDR are to all of us today.

Familiar topics

Shakespeare's writing was strongly influenced early in his career by **Christopher Marlowe**, the dominant author in Elizabethan drama at the time. Marlowe had a gift for writing powerful rhetoric and a gift for applying irony to his subjects. Shakespeare took Marlowe's approach and broadened it. **History plays** as a genre were very popular in the last couple of decades of the 1500s, and as a genre, there were recognisable themes and structures:

Influenced by Marlowe

> "The main themes behind Shakespeare's histories are the main themes of Tudor political thought – kingship, the sinfulness of

3.5 Notes on themes

rebellion against God's deputy on earth, the problems arising from royal misgovernment."[7]

Abuse of royal power

Also important is the point that the history plays were not exclusively seen as entertainment: "The precedent of reconstructing the past as a warning mirror for the present"[8] places the subject matter of the history plays in a more universal context. This means for example that the character of Richard in *Richard III* is not only portrayed and seen by the audience as a unique human being, an individual character: in addition, **the figure of Richard represents a moral story arc** which illustrates the consequences of immoral acts, in particular, the abuse of royal power.

> **Morality plays:** These allegorical dramas were most popular in Europe during the 15th and 16th centuries. They followed a simple and consistent structure: a protagonist encounters various embodiments of moral values (for example, the protagonist meets a character called Knowledge or Discretion, who represents the specific virtue in action and speech). These incarnated moral values attempt to persuade the protagonist to follow the true moral path, and not to be led into temptation by their opposites, the sins and immoral values (i.e. greed, adultery, pride etc.).

---

[7] Boris Ford. *The Pelican Guide to English Literature. Volume 2: The Age of Shakespeare.* p. 62.
[8] Ibid. p. 62

3.5 Notes on themes

> The morality plays appear to have been highly influential, to judge simply by their popularity, and we can find traces of their established literary techniques, moral-artistic goals and pedagogical intentions in more structurally and thematically sophisticated dramas, such as those of Marlowe or Shakespeare.

This "universalisation" of his fictionalised historical characters is not exclusive to Shakespeare, it was **an accepted technique found in contemporary historical dramas**. Where his innovations and genius become ever clearer is in his ability to sharpen this morality play *functionality* of a character while at the same time creating complex and fully rounded human characters. Richard is here both a symbolic, universal warning of the consequences of immorality, and a believable, multi-layered individual, vibrantly and entertainingly alive.

On the role of the protagonist in Shakespeare's history plays:

„Was diese zehn Stücke [the history plays] von den Tragödien unterscheidet, ist nicht einfach das Thema der eigenen nationalen Vorgeschichte, sondern die unterschiedliche Fokussierung: Steht in den Tragödien der Protagonist im Zentrum, so wird in den Historien gerade die Interdependenz von Herrscherindividuum und politischen Strukturen thematisch. Menschliches Fehlverhalten wird hier immer auch in seinen politischen Bedingungen und Folgen gezeigt, und das Ringen des Individuums

Hans Ulrich Seeber

3.5 Notes on themes

um Identität ist immer auch ein Ringen um politische Autorität und nationale Identität."[9]

The themes of *Richard III*

Richard is the absolutely dominant character in the play. No other figure even comes close to stealing the spotlight from him. It is not surprising to find that the play's themes are all focussed on his actions and personality. These themes are:

- → Morality, immorality and the moral laws of the Tudor universe
- → Ambition (as a destructive force when uncoupled from morality)
- → The nature of power (and its moral/theological character)
- → The abuse of power
- → Fate, free will and fatalism (including the supernatural elements of the play)

Because so many of the themes are so densely interconnected, we shall look at them in three groups: Morality – Ambition & power – Fate & free will.

Morality, immorality and the laws

Richard and Richmond

From the opening of the play, we know that we will be following the career of a man who has intentionally chosen to behave in an immoral manner in order to satisfy his desires and ambitions. His evil is enjoyable for the audience, but the moral laws of Shakespeare's literary and political world cannot allow a monster like Richard to

---

[9] Hans Ulrich Seeber: *Englische Literaturgeschichte*. p. 130.

3.5 Notes on themes

rampage without facing the consequences of his challenges to the moral order. So there must be a moral force to counter his evil: a force with broader vision than that of Richard, who is laser-focussed on his personal ambitions and utterly uninterested in anything else. This force is manifested in the character of **Richmond**, who leads the rebellion against Richard as king and finally kills him in battle.

But even though we can look at this moral symmetry as if it were something purely historical, at heart it has similarities with the cliché "Be nice to the people you meet on your way up – they're the people you'll meet on your way down"[10]. This succinct nugget of advice combines **the moral lesson** with an earthy dose of common sense, a mixture of which Shakespeare would surely have approved.

Because the play would have had a relatable, contemporary relevance for Shakespeare's audiences, **the question of morality** exists within the text of the play, independent of where and when it is being staged, with a life of its own as a literary, dramatic technique; and also in a much more immediate way for Shakespeare's contemporaries. This is again an example of how *Richard III* can have both specific and universal meaning and relevance.

Shakespeare's audiences

The broad moral character of Richard and his actions can be identified all through the play with specific examples of him using the tools of immorality – such as **hypocrisy, manipulation and deceit** – in his grasp for power.

---

10 It's not entirely clear who coined this phrase, but its oldest known usage was apparently in 1932. https://quoteinvestigator.com/2010/10/16/be-nice-on-way-up/

3.5 Notes on themes

TEXT	REFERENCE	NOTES
[...] I am subtle, false, and treacherous.	I.1.37	Right from the opening of the play, Richard shows us his true colours. He is deliberately taking the immoral course to power.
[...] this deep disgrace in brotherhood / Touches me deeper than you can imagine.	I.1.111–112	Richard often employs hypocrisy to deceive people around him. Here, he is pretending grief for the imprisonment of his brother Clarence – which is the result of his own plots.
[...] With lies well steel'd with weighty arguments;	I.1.147	In the early scenes of the play, Richard often tells us in asides like this example what his strategy will be and how he plans to make his next move.
I'll have her; but I'll not keep her long.	I.2.231	Richard delights in having overwhelmed Lady Anne, who hates him with a passion, with his own seductive rhetoric, but as soon as he is alone on stage he reminds us that Anne is nothing more than a stepping stone for him on his path to power: he has absolutely no interest in the woman beyond her temporary usefulness.
They do me wrong, and I will not endure it [...]. Because I cannot flatter and speak fair, [...] I must be held a rancorous enemy.	I.3.42–50	This is a good example of Richard's moral slipperiness, and Shakespeare's irony. Claiming to be victimised because of his ugliness, Richard has taken his own motivation (to seize power because he is not pretty and suited for courtly harmony, as laid out in the play's opening speech) and turned it inside out in order to attack his opponents.

3.5 Notes on themes

TEXT	REFERENCE	NOTES
I am too childish-foolish for this world.	I.3.142	As he often does during the play, Richard is here pretending to be less than he is: less dangerous, less powerful, less clever. He is a wolf in sheep's clothing, as moments like this show us.
[Richard expresses regret for his part in the deaths which have grieved old Queen Margaret]	I.3.304–319	Richard displays remorse here for having caused the old queen so much trouble and heartache, and reminds the other nobles that their gain had been at her cost. This is all true, and it is an interestingly ambiguous scene: Richard is praised by the others for his Christian spirit, and mutters in a bitter aside that the time is not yet right for him to attack. And yet there is nothing false or dishonest about his recognition that he and the others have all contributed to the deep pain that has driven the old queen to curse them all.
[Richard enters, being carried high between two bishops.] MAYOR: See, where his grace stands 'tween two clergymen. BUCKINGHAM: Two props of virtue for a Christian prince […].	III.7.94–95	There is a pun in here on prop, as in support, and prop, as in theatrical property – items used on stage. This is a wonderfully substantial pun. At a point in the play in which Richard is about to make his final lunge for the throne, this shows the world that he is a Christian prince, a good man, and that he is supported by high-ranking Church representatives. It also tells us the exact opposite: Richard is about as Christian as his heraldic beast, the boar, and the two bishops are indeed props, colourful distractors he can wave around to persuade others that he is something he is not.

3.5 Notes on themes

"The worm of conscience still begnaw thy soul!" (I.3.222)

Richard is not amoral

Margaret is cursing Richard. This is an important aspect of her curses: she believes that Richard has some remnants of a conscience left in him, and that these remnants will haunt and torment him. Richard is not some beast raging and killing for the joy of it: he is not amoral. He knows perfectly well what is right and what is wrong, and so **he is immoral**. Being a human being with a moral sense, therefore, he is not unaware of the corruption of his soul as he follows his career of evil.

Betrayal

The topic of betrayal is linked to all other themes. It is an immoral act, typically, and it happens often within the play in the service of ambition and the lust for power. Betrayal can be real, as with Richard's betrayal of pretty much everyone he comes into contact with, and an illusion. The latter is the case with Richard's sudden and irrational fear that Buckingham is going to turn against him, because his closest advisor and ally seemed concerned by Richard's commands to have the young princes in the Tower murdered (Act IV Scene 2). When Richard says:

> "The deep-revolving witty Buckingham
> No more shall be the neighbour to my counsel.
> Hath he so long held out with me untir'd,
> And stops he now for breath? well, be it so."
> (Lines 42–45)

Richard and Buckingham

Richard's paranoia is making him mad. Here again is a self-fulfilling prophecy, though, because Buckingham understands perfectly well that the slightest suspicion in Richard's mind can trigger an assassination. So as soon as Buckingham's reticence to kill children is seen

3.5 Notes on themes

by Richard, the vicious cycle begins: **Richard doubts Buckingham, Buckingham feels insecure,** Richard interprets insecurity as untrustworthiness, and paranoia takes over. When Buckingham tries to remind Richard of the rewards he had been offered he is ignored (IV.2.82–121) until he finally understands that Richard is going to betray him, too: "And is it thus? repays he my deep service / With such contempt? made I him king for this?" (IV.2.118–119) We can see here that Buckingham feels not only fear that he will be killed, or anger that he is not being granted the rewards he was promised: **he feels betrayed**. He has stuck with Richard loyally through some pretty troubling episodes, and now he too is being cut loose.

This scene covers another example of betrayal, when Richard orders Catesby to begin spreading **rumours that his wife Anne is unwell** (IV.2.46-65). Richard plots to kill Anne and marry his own niece.

Lady Anne

He reflects on the murderous betrayal of everyone around him, noting that "Tear-falling pity dwells not in this eye" (IV.2.65).

Ambition & power

Ambition is a great motivating force for a plot because (like for example revenge) it implies a specific goal, an arc for the story to follow. The ambition on display in *Richard III* is interestingly complex because it is born (see the opening speech by Richard) from a dark and dangerous instinct, namely Richard's desire to basically **take revenge on the world** because he is physically and morally deformed.

The destructive impulse of Richard's ambition

At the beginning of the play, Richard himself comments on how peaceful and relaxed the state of the country has become following recent military conflicts. He speaks about the "glorious summer" of

3.5 Notes on themes

the time, with "all the clouds" being banished (see I.1.2–3). The battles are over, the weapons have been put away, people are laughing and dancing once again.

So if everything is so relaxed and harmonious, and everybody is running around falling in love and dancing, where does the plot, the story, the conflict come from?

Richard's personal problem

"I am determined to prove a villain" – this is the key moment (I.1.30). Richard tells us, the audience, that because his deformed body and twisted nature, his insecurity and self-loathing, have combined to make him **a permanent outsider in this current happy England**, he has decided – intentionally, maliciously – to compensate for what he feels he is being excluded from by evil acts (this is also the **key moment for the theme of fate & free will**, see below in this chapter).

Richard's ambition is a powerful force. It is what drives the plot of the play. What we see from the beginning is that this ambition is utterly corrupted by Richard's immoral impulses.

TEXT	REFERENCE	NOTES
I am determined to prove a villain […].	I.1.30	Richard's opening speech gives us the context for what is to come, and gives us a glimpse into the mind of a man whose ambition is intrinsically dangerous and immoral. Richard is already laying plots to ruin his brothers as he begins to make his way to the throne.
Clarence still breathes; Edward still lives and reigns: / When they are gone, then must I count my gains.	I.1.160–161	Here we can see Richard's cold arithmetic of ambition. He gains when others lose: he progresses by walking over (having killed) those in his way – even his own brothers.

3.5 Notes on themes

TEXT	REFERENCE	NOTES
Poor painted queen [...]! / Why strew'st thou sugar on that bottled spider, / Whose deadly web ensnareth thee about?	I.3.241–243	Old Queen Margaret, here addressing Queen Elizabeth, warns her of the danger posed by Richard (the spider). Margaret can see Richard's deadly ambition, and she can see how ill-prepared the nobles around him are to deal with it. She understands that Richard's intelligence and power is not held back by any moral or decent impulse, his ambition is lethal.
Fool, fool! thou whet'st a knife to kill thyself.	I.3.244	In the same speech, Margaret is even more explicit about the danger Richard poses for his enemies. Any support for Richard, she is saying, is a terrible idea, because he is coming to defeat and dominate everyone.
O Buckingham! take heed of yonder dog: / Look, when he fawns, he bites; and when he bites, / His venom tooth will rankle to the death: / Have not to do with him, beware of him; [...].	I.3.289–292	Old Queen Margaret also addresses Buckingham, an ally of Richard. This particular moment is important as later, when her warning has come true for Buckingham, he remembers what she had said, and regrets not having heeded her, because his loyalty to the "dog" with "venom tooth" (Richard) costs him his life.
O! full of danger is the Duke of Gloucester!	II.3.27	This comment by a citizen on the street comes during a conversation about the state of the realm. Richard is a polarizing figure, and many people, even just random guys on the street, worry that he is a dangerous man to be trusted with power.

3.5 Notes on themes

Power

Richard is seeking power: he wants to rule England. His ambition is, as we have seen, **corrupted by his selfish and wicked nature**. In smaller examples we can often see how Richard wields his power over those below him, and how he uses the existing power structures – feudal, dynastic power bases and the complex temporary ebb and flow of favour and loyalty.

TEXT	REFERENCE	NOTES
Unmanner'd dog! stand thou when I command: [...].	I.2.39	Here is Richard in typically tyrannical mode, ordering the men bearing the corpse of King Henry VI. When still just a Duke, he can't conceal what kind of person he is when he has power over someone else.
[...] the world is grown so bad / That wrens make prey where eagles dare not perch: / Since every Jack became a gentleman / There's many a gentle person made a Jack.	I.3.70–73	Challenging Queen Elizabeth and her followers, Richard implies that they are not really nobility, but that they are commoners (common little wrens, as opposed to noble eagles) who have been advanced in society too far. This is Richard playing politics: he is seeking to undermine any potential opponents' legitimacy, while manoeuvring to solidify his own through murder and marriage.
Small joy have I in being England's queen.	I.3.110	Queen Elizabeth here articulates a weariness with power that is surprisingly rarely heard in the play. Power doesn't seem to be enjoyable, safe or easy to survive in this world, and this poor woman has suffered more than enough from insults, conspiracies and dangerous jealousies.

3.5 Notes on themes

TEXT	REFERENCE	NOTES
[Richard arguing with Elizabeth and her loyal nobles]	I.3.113–154	Richard dives here into the complicated and confusing dynastic politics and struggles of recent years. He attempts to show that Elizabeth and her friends are not only not really noble, but that they were also untrustworthy, having fought on and supported Lancaster against York.
We follow'd then our lord, our lawful king; / So should we you, if you should be our king.	I.3.147–148	Lord Rivers here counters Richard's attacks, providing a basic and reasonable justification for what their loyalties had been during the last few years. Allegiance to the reigning monarch was extremely important: rebellion is more than a political act, it is understood to be an existential challenge to the order of the universe.
[Richard and his closest allies discuss political strategies]	III.1.151–200	Acquiring power in a feudal hierarchy means not striking at those above you until you are sure of the support of those around you. Richard needs the Duke of Buckingham, and so he promises to reward him richly for his support. Here we can see how Richard plots with his allies, as he, Catesby and Buckingham discuss the potential loyalty of other nobles, including Hastings, the Lord Chamberlain. This is power politics at work.
[Richard and Buckingham plot to trick the Lord Mayor of London into supporting Richard's claim for the throne]	III.5	Richard and Buckingham play a complex charade here to deceive the Mayor into thinking that London was in grave danger, and that Richard has saved it. At the same time, Buckingham is sent out to spread rumours about the illegitimacy of dead king Edward's children. These tactics serve to disorient everyone else and cast doubt on the validity of others' claim to the throne.

3.5 Notes on themes

TEXT	REFERENCE	NOTES
Let not the heavens hear these tell-tale women / Rail on the Lord's anointed.	IV.4.150–151	Richard responds here to the curses and accusations being flung at him by his mother (the Duchess of York) and Queen Elizabeth. He is demanding that he should not have to put up with anything because he is the "Lord's anointed" – as King, that is, he is divinely appointed. These less-divine creatures should not dare to insult or attack him, he is saying.

Act II Scene 1: Hypocrisy in power

Richard and Elizabeth: each with their factions of loyal nobles

In this scene, Richard and Queen Elizabeth face off in court in front of the sick and ailing King Edward IV, each with their factions of loyal nobles. **This scene is about politics and the performance of politics**. When the gathered nobles promise to be great friends from now on, at Edward's insistence, they all do so with flowery speeches. But this is entirely hollow gesturing, a pantomime to appease the king.

Richard fits right in here. Everyone present is pretending; and he is the master. When he says, "'Tis death to me to be at enmity; / I hate it, and desire all good men's love" (II.1.61–62) he is joining in the general chorus of loudly proclaimed peace and harmony, but we by this point know very well that this is just hypocritical nonsense on his part. Everyone places a great deal of value on what other people say in public, it seems, but Richard has understood that it doesn't matter one way or another – **you say what needs to be said in order to help yourself**.

We often see Richard and his followers being hypocrites, so this is a nice opportunity to be able to see basically everyone being sanctimonious, shallow hypocrites. As King Edward dies before the

3.5 Notes on themes

next scene, we soon learn how much these promises made to keep the peace are actually worth (not much: Richard and Buckingham have Elizabeth's supporters imprisoned by the opening of Act II Scene 4).

> **Feudal titles**: The power structure of Tudor England is of course quite different from our current parliamentary democracy. Here is a brief overview of the different titles within the hierarchy of English and European monarchical and feudal society:
> → **The King / The Queen**: The ruler of the country, the absolute power. The position of King or Queen is believed to be by the grace of God: divinely ordained.
> → **Archduke / Archduchess**: This powerful title was historically used by the Habsburg dynasty, rulers of the Archduchy of Austria.
> → **Grand Prince / Grand Princess**: Also known as Grand Duke / Duchess, these are royal children of a monarch who rule territories.
> → **Prince / Princess:** The children of the monarch. In *Richard III* we have several princes, all of whom are seen as enemies by Richard because of their legitimate legal claims to the throne he is seeking to take for himself.
> → **Duke / Duchess:** Richard is Duke of Gloucester when we first meet him. His younger brother is Duke of Clarence; their elder brother is king. The mother of the three men is the Duchess of York.
> → **Marquess / Marchioness:** We have one Marquess in *Richard III*, the Marquess of Dorset.

3.5 Notes on themes

> → **Count / Countess / Earl:** Richard's final nemesis Richmond is an Earl, as is his stepfather Lord Stanley, Earl of Derby.
> → **Viscount / Viscountess**
> → **Baron / Baroness**
> → **Knight / Lord / Lady:** These lesser nobles were the lower ranks of the peerage (the system of hereditary noble ranks). Knights and Lords own land and castles and serfs (peasants), but are much less powerful politically than the higher-ranked nobles.

The abuse of power

This topic is quite complicated in *Richard III*. We are reminded frequently during the early scenes that rebellion against the rightful monarch is a terrible thing, not only because of the civil unrest it provokes, but because **it threatens the divine order of things**. But then towards the end of the play we have righteous Richmond leading a rebellion against King Richard III, and in doing so restoring health and peace and harmony to the country.

Richmond's rebellion is morally justified

The reason Richmond's rebellion is morally justified is because **Richard has abused his power** to an unbearable degree. He seized the throne through murder (including infanticide) and deceit: he is so evil that he has become an illegitimate king. We saw him already as a nobleman in the early scenes behaving badly towards his inferiors, and that aspect of his character has not changed.

Hastings' execution

In the short scene Act III Scene 4, a scribe speaks about the obvious wrongness of the warrant for Hastings' execution. This is an indictment of Richard's abuse of his power: we know, having heard the plotting, how unjust his death was, and now we have an

3.5 Notes on themes

impartial outsider openly confirming what we know to be **a lethal injustice**.

The illegitimacy of Richard's claim to power, combined with his ambition to force this claim by any means necessary, means of course that he is abusing power simply by possessing it: he has no right to it, he takes it any way by duplicitous means, and **murders his way up the ladder of power**. He is rejected by specific nobles throughout his ascent, and when at a key point he starts to test how the citizens of London feel about him, he learns (through the Lord Mayor and Buckingham) that the populace is pretty sceptical of his claim.

Once he has ascended the throne, **Richard begins to lose all control over his murderous passions**. What had been ambition is now paranoia: the first thing he does on taking the throne is to suggest to Buckingham that the young princes in the Tower should be murdered. Buckingham pretends not to understand, forcing Richard to say, "Shall I be plain? I wish the bastards dead; / And I would have it suddenly perform'd" (IV.2.18–19). This is the most blatant example to date of Richard's murderous tactics. No longer concealed by careful metaphors and insinuations, but explicitly **commanded**. Richard has absolutely become the villain he promised us he would be. Power, for him, is not the health of the realm and the well-being of his people: it is a **sleepless, paranoid nightmare of revenge and infanticide**.

Richard's murderous tactics

Fate & free will

If there are forces beyond our control directing the course of our lives, can there ever really be such a thing as free will? This is one of the biggest questions we can ask ourselves. It plays a role in *Richard III* because of the sense of divine retribution in the way that **immoral behaviour brings its own punishment**, and in Richard

3.5 Notes on themes

taking his physical and moral deformity as a sign that he was never supposed to be good: that he is built for evil, predestined, unable to steer against his designated fate.

The justice of fate?

There is a sense of almost karmic justice in the complete destruction Richard suffers as a result of the actions he has taken. He brings it upon himself. There are a number of curses flying around during the play, most importantly and powerfully the curses of old Queen Margaret (see Act I Scene 3).

Divine justice

With his increasing power, Richard's personality seems to begin to fracture and crumble. He becomes paranoid and tight-lipped, hard to recognise as the same man who in the early scenes was overwhelming others with his hypnotic, poisonous rhetoric. By the end of the play he has lost everything and has been punished with **death on the battlefield** for his tyrannical and murderous deeds. The universe, in the form of divine justice, has reasserted the proper order of things by putting Richmond on the throne and freeing the country from the terrors of Richard.

Dreams, prophecies, curses and ghosts

Supernatural elements

From old Queen Margaret's fearsome curses to dreams of a boar (Richard's heraldic animal) and the visitation of ghosts, both benign and malevolent, there are whispers and hints of the supernatural throughout *Richard III*. These elements are used by Shakespeare to reinforce **specific moral lessons**, beyond the cause-and-effect justice of Richard's eventual downfall, and can be understood as being

→ primarily, literary techniques to highlight these moral questions, and
→ secondarily, exciting and chilling "special effects" intended to crank up the atmosphere and intensity of the entertainment.

3.5 Notes on themes

TEXT	REFERENCE	NOTES
He hearkens after prophecies and dreams;	I.1.54	Richard's younger brother Clarence, arrested and being led to the Tower, is talking about their elder brother, King Edward. The "prophecies" he is talking about are not in the slightest supernatural or genuine – they are the flowers of Richard's lies and plots, which have taken root in the court and created an atmosphere of paranoia.
Long mayst thou live to wail thy children's loss [...].	I.3.204	This is merely one of the many, many curses Margaret fires off at Richard and his followers, and Queen Elizabeth and her supporters.
Thy friends suspect for traitors while thou livest / And take deep traitors for thy dearest friends!	I.3.223–224	More of Margaret's curses, this time aimed specifically at Richard. This one is worth remembering, as later scenes in the play find him growing increasingly paranoid and living out exactly what Margaret cursed him with: an inability to recognise true friends, and a reliance on individuals who are neither loyal nor reliable. This curse feeds Richard's paranoia, and becomes in effect a self-fulfilling prophecy, paranoia being a state of mind that by definition forces the paranoid individual to see the world through a warped lens.
Now Margaret's curse is fall'n upon our heads [...].	III.3.14	Lord Grey here gives the first, and far from last, reminder of old Queen Margaret's powerful curses from earlier.
O Margaret, Margaret! now thy heavy curse / Is lighted on poor Hastings' wretched head.	III.4.92–93	Hastings is the next victim of Richard's murderous ambition to recall the old woman's curses.

3.5 Notes on themes

TEXT	REFERENCE	NOTES
[The ghosts visit Richard and Richmond on the eve of the battle]	Act V Scene 3 (from line 119 on)	This is an interesting split-screen episode in the play. Both Richard and Richmond are visited by the same sequence of ghosts, who address both men, cursing and damning Richard and offering encouragement and support for Richmond. This scene suggests supernatural forces beyond the mundane dreams of people: the ghosts and their messages are like signals sent by a power of universal justice (perhaps God) to assist Richmond in restoring order to the country and rescuing the throne from Richard's tyrannical abuses of power.

3.6 Style and language

> **SUMMARY**
>
> It is important to look at two particular aspects of the language Shakespeare uses in *Richard III*:
> → At Richard's **powers of persuasion** and the techniques of deception and seduction.
> → And at **the rich black humour** of the play, which gives the story of evil, ambition and murder a refreshing, modern, ironic layer.
>
> Other interesting aspects include **boar imagery** and the extremity of **the curses** and insults used in the play.

Rhetoric

The play opens with Richard arguing why he has chosen to follow the path of evil and deception to pursue his ambitions. He is alone on stage, which in a play means that the character is alone and what they are saying is an inner monologue, the sound of a mind talking to itself. **And we see here the core of his personality**: he is a cynical, clever, unscrupulous man who has no illusions about himself and nothing but contempt for the people around him. We as an audience can eavesdrop on Richard's plotting and goals – unlike characters on stage with him later, we are shown the real thing.

Richard's inner monologue (Act I)

During the play, and in the first half in particular, we see Richard using his **rhetorical skills to overwhelm others**. It should be remembered that Richard's rhetoric is consistently boosted by hypocrisy and untruthfulness. One of the most important examples is his lengthy interaction with Anne (I.2), which begins with her wishing him dead and ends with them apparently about to get married. Even Richard is a bit taken aback by how easy it was (see

Richard's rhetoric

3.6 Style and language

his speech at the end of the scene). It is hard for us to have much sympathy with Anne after she given in so easily to Richard. Later, she comments on this: "Within so small a time, my woman's heart / Grossly grew captive to his honey words" (IV.1 78–79). Richard had already been surprised at how quickly he had broken down her defences, and we as an audience were also a little nonplussed, and now the victim of Richard's rhetoric sees clearly that she had been weak and given in too easily to flattery.

Richard abuses his fellows

Anne of course has absolutely no value for Richard other than as **a steppingstone on his way to the throne.** At the earliest possible opportunity, he plans get rid of her and replace her with another wife even closer to the throne, to enhance his own claim to the crown.

This plotline gives us more of Richard's agile and utterly **unscrupulous rhetorical skills**. In Act IV Scene 4, when he is already crowned king, he is confronted by the Duchess of York and Queen Elizabeth. Both women curse him. His mother leaves, and he remains onstage with Queen Elizabeth. And now he asks her about her daughter, also called Elizabeth. The queen loathes Richard, she wishes him dead, and she is incredulous when he asks her for her help in wooing her daughter (his niece). We can see here how **Richard is utterly unbothered by moral questions** (like, how will the young Elizabeth react to marrying the man who murdered almost all of the male members of her family?), and seeks to overcome any obstacles by clever rhetoric – for example, "If I did take the kingdom from your sons, / To make amends I'll give it to your daughter" (IV.4.295–296).

Act IV, 4

And again, as with the earlier scene with Anne, once he has finally bludgeoned the suspicious and righteously furious woman into agreeing to his plans, Richard is both surprised and contemptuous of how easily she has given in: "Relenting fool, and shallow, chang-

3.6 Style and language

ing woman" (IV.4.432) are his words when she leaves him. Richard proves again and again that **he has no respect for anybody**, least of all for those who succumb to his rhetoric.

Black comedy

Richard III is at times a very funny play. It is definitely not a comedy: but watching a clever, eloquent and utterly immoral man challenging the world can be extremely entertaining. Shakespeare, as is often the case, makes **frequent use of puns and word play**. At the very beginning of the play we have the sun/son play on words and imagery, and this kind of wordplay can be found throughout the text. There are also more elaborate puns like Catesby's "The princes both make high account of you / [*Aside*] For they account his head high on the bridge" (III.2.69–70).

Entertaining

Some exchanges between characters are comical, **despite their morbid or tragic content**. Much humour is derived from the inability of some characters to see or understand Richard's duplicity. When Lord Hastings, for example, who has been consistently played and manipulated by Buckingham, Richard and others, says of Richard "I think there's never a man in Christendom / Can lesser hide his love or hate than he" (III.4.51–52) it's hard not to burst out laughing.

The irony of many situations and events within the play provides a further level of cerebral humour to a play which often gleefully splashes around in the entertaining muck of insult comedy (see for example Anne's attacks on Richard in Act I Scene 2).

Irony

Competitive grief

On two occasions, the women who are grieving for their fathers, husbands and sons (and the children of those murdered men) meet on stage together to compare the tragedies that have afflicted them, and despite their great grief, odd moments of humour arise. The

3.6 Style and language

fact that so many of the characters have the same name gives an absurd edge to expressions of "competitive grief" amongst the noblewomen and children.

From Act II Scene 2 (lines 72–79):
Children: Ah for our father, for our dear Lord Clarence!
Duchess of York: Alas! for both, both mine, Edward and Clarence!
Queen Elizabeth: What stay had I but Edward? and he's gone.
Children: What stay had we but Clarence? and he's gone.
Duchess of York: What stays had I but they? and they are gone.
Queen Elizabeth: Was never widow had so dear a loss.
Children: Were never orphans had so dear a loss.
Duchess of York: Was never mother had so dear a loss.

And from Act IV Scene 4 (lines 39–46):
Margaret: Tell o'er your woes again by viewing mine.
I had an Edward, till a Richard kill'd him;
I had a Harry, till a Richard kill'd him.
Thou hadst an Edward, till a Richard kill'd him;
Thou hadst a Richard, till a Richard kill'd him.
Duchess of York: I had a Richard too, and thou didst kill him;
    I had a Rutland too, thou holp'st to kill him.
Margaret: Thou hadst a Clarence too, and Richard kill'd him.

Repetition

In both these examples we can see a lot of **repetition being used** – not just repetition of the names, but of the sentences. The effect is weirdly comical, and both scenes have a sense of grief arithmetic, as if the women (and children) are adding up their grievances to see who has been hurt most by Richard. The first example above in particular has a very odd competitive feeling to it.

3.6 Style and language

Boar imagery

Richard of Gloucester's heraldic beast – the symbol of his family – was the boar. Boars are basically tougher, scarier versions of farm pigs, but we can see in the use of boar and pig imagery and jokes throughout the play that the pig and its relatives are subject to the same abuse they always have been throughout history and around the world. We may love to eat pork and bacon, but we all tend to view pigs as greedy, dirty beasts.

Symbol of Richard's family

Here are some examples of **boar imagery** as used through the play.

TEXT	REFERENCE	NOTES
Thou elvish-mark'd, abortive, rooting hog!	I.3.228	Margaret slips in this insult during her lengthy cursing of Richard and his allies. She compares him here to an ugly hog digging around in the dirt.
The wretched, bloody and usurping boar [...].	V.2.7	On the eve of the great battle at the end of the play, this is how Richmond describes Richard.
He dreamt the boar had razed off his helm: [...]. Stanley did dream the boar did raise our helm	III.2.11 / III.4.81	These two quotations show the dream that Stanley had of a boar beheading him and Hastings: the first is the report of the dream, the second the dreadful realisation that the dream is coming true.
To fly the boar before the boar pursues / Were to incense the boar to follow us / And make pursuit where he did mean no chase.	III.2.28–30	Hastings here suggests that running away from Richard will simply draw his attention and trigger more danger.

3.6 Style and language

TEXT	REFERENCE	NOTES
[...] where is your boar-spear, man? / Fear you the boar, and go so unprovided?	III.2.72–73	Hastings addresses Stanley.

Extreme language and imagery

Aversion

Much of the language used by characters around Richard to express their hatred of the man and horror at his actions is undeniably extreme. **Lady Anne, for example**, the Prince of Wales' widow and later Richard's wife, curses her husband's murderer (I.2.13–28) with **intense and frightening imagery**, and when in the same scene Richard appears, she becomes even more direct and extreme in her choice of insults. Here are some of the ways she addresses and describes Richard in this scene (line number provided, all examples from **Act I Scene 2**):

→ fiend 34
→ the devil 45
→ minister of hell 46
→ Foul devil 50
→ ... thou hast made the happy earth thy hell 51
→ ... thou lump of foul deformity 57
→ Villain 70
→ ... diffus'd infection of a man 78
→ devilish slave 90
→ He is in heaven, where thou shalt never come. 107
→ And thou unfit for any place but hell. 110
→ homicide 126
→ thou dost infect mine eyes. 148

3.6 Style and language

The hatred which is expressed in such extreme language is, surprisingly, overcome by Richard's deceitful rhetoric – in the same scene, astonishingly. The comparative ease with which Richard wins her over, given the extreme nature of the words she throws at him, raises again the idea that at the end of the day, **words mean nothing**. This troubling idea can be seen at several points in the play, where the cheapness and irrelevance of words spoken by characters is silhouetted against the true nature behind: **words are a game, they are used to deflect suspicion or to sow evil plot**s, they are used to make others believe whatever you want them to believe – they are fundamentally untrustworthy.

Only actions matter, and it is only words-as-action – curses – that have meaning beyond the instant in which they are spoken. Promises are broken (for example, Richard's promise to reward Buckingham for his loyalty and support), loyalty and fidelity have no more inherent value than opinions, and the deceitful difference between what a person says and does and what that person thinks and plans is constantly on full view as **Richard lies and deceives his way through England to seize the throne**.

Only actions matter

3.7 Interpretations

3.7 Interpretations

SUMMARY

Richard III remains both popular and relevant: it is entertaining, and it manages to explore the themes of ambition, abuse of power and the justice of fate in ways which continue to speak to us hundreds of years later in very different political and social circumstances.

Power and manipulation

Elizabethan era

Politically, the play is set in (and was written during) **an age of feudal, royal power**, in which the country is ruled by a monarch with absolute power. The general assumption was that the King or Queen of England rules by the grace of God: that royalty was divinely appointed, and that God was on the side of the righteous.

This idealistic concept is harshly contradicted by the events of *Richard III* (and British history in general): as we can see in this play, taking the crown of England has little or nothing to do with the righteousness of God and the divine suitability of the monarch, and everything to do with **power** and manipulation. It is not difficult to draw parallels with our own age, where democracy – the free expression of the political will of the citizens – is an ideal equivalent to the divine righteousness of a monarch blessed by God, and the **abuse of power** and manipulation of the machines of power in Richard's era is comparable to what we have today: the manipulation and corruption of information and the truth, and the weaponization of fear and bigotry. Any society, at any time, can see in *Richard III* reflections of contemporary abuse of power.

The play has remained popular and has been regularly performed on stage in the centuries since it was written. In the 20th century

3.7 Interpretations

Al Pacino and Winona Ryder in *Looking for Richard* (1996).
© picture alliance/ United Archives/ kpa Publicity

there were also **several film adaptations**, more or less faithful to the text of Shakespeare's play, notably a 1955 film starring Laurence Olivier, and an adaptation in 1995. The 1995 version starred Ian McKellen (familiar to 21st century audiences as Gandalf in *The Lord of the Rings* and Magneto in the *X-Men* films) and was interestingly updated to be set in a fictional fascist England in the 1930s.

Al Pacino's *Looking for Richard*
And besides all of the more or less conventional adaptations of the play for film or television (or radio), the legendary American actor

3.7 Interpretations

Al Pacino – many films since the late 1960s, including *The Godfather* parts 1, 2 and 3 (1972, 1974, 1990) and *Scarface* (1983) – released a film in 1996 called *Looking for Richard*.

Looking for Richard

This strange and fascinating film is not a feature film, as had been intended, but instead **a kind of documentary film** about how the initial film project failed, including investigations into how relevant Shakespeare and his masterpieces have remained and found their way into contemporary popular culture.

The film includes scenes of conventional acting, with **Pacino** playing Richard, and the rest of the cast including other hugely famous and successful actors: for example, **Kevin Spacey** (*LA Confidential* 1997; *House of Cards* (Netflix) 2013–2018, *Horrible Bosses* 2011, *Horrible Bosses 2* 2014) played Richmond, and **Winona Ryder** (*Heathers* 1988, *Bram Stoker's Dracula* 1992, *Stranger Things* (Netflix) 2016–) played Lady Anne.

Shakespeare for today

Pacino set out to show audiences that Shakespeare is not intimidating (due to the difficulty of the language), or boring, or irrelevant[11]. His primary goal was to make Shakespeare live: "Shakespeare's text is meant to be performed; it is a living, breathing thing in the mouths of actors from generation to generation."[12]

---

11   http://www.americanpopularculture.com/archive/film/pacino_shakespeare.htm
12   Ibid.

4. RECEPTION

SUMMARY

> As is the case with many of Shakespeare's plays, *Richard III* has remained a popular and critically admired work from its first performance.

The themes of ambition and the abuse of power, the extraordinary central character, and the rich, funny language have all contributed to the enduring success of the play. Audiences all around the world and throughout history **can identify with the story** of a greedy, evil man who murders and lies his way to power only to be confronted with the consequences of his evil actions. It's a story with universal appeal, and not only for contemporary audiences, for whom the English dynastic wars were still memory rather than history. In the early 21st century we in the modern world can still see parallels with the vulnerability of our own democratic processes and **the abuse of power by immoral or unscrupulous figures**.

Following Shakespeare's death (1616), performances of his plays began to suffer. **Many of the plays were cut** to make them faster and less demanding. In the last years of the 17th century, **women were allowed for the first time to play roles on stage**, and this led to some plays being re-written or adapted to enlarge female roles or invent new ones. It has been noted that during the 18th century and into the 19th, "[t]hose who really appreciated Shakespeare usually stayed away from the theatre".[13]

The fall and rise in respect for Shakespeare's art

---

[13] All quotations and references here from: Muir, Kenneth: *Changing Interpretations of Shakespeare*. In: Ford (ed.): The Age of Shakespeare. p. 282–301.

While performances appear to have suffered for a very long period following his death, appreciation of his work as a poet and writer, rather than as a "content provider" for the stage, remained evident. The audience of those willing and able to appreciate Shakespeare's genius had always been there.

This was to change however with the spread of schools and public education. Suddenly, **generations were being taught Shakespeare's language** and were compelled to come to grips with the rich treasure chest of his ideas and artistic genius. This was a development that made Shakespeare less intimidating for the general population, which, in conjunction with the spread of more sophisticated staging techniques (including developments such as electric lighting), **made Shakespeare's works on stage as popular as he had ever been**.

Critical responses to Shakespeare

In addition, critical responses to Shakespeare had gone through different phases. He was dismissed by many critics in the 17th and 18th centuries as **being too melodramatic, not precise enough**, having no real knowledge of Classical (Ancient Greek or Roman) sources, and he was dismissed by many because his writing did not conform to contemporary fashions in poetry and the theatre.

But there were always critics and other writers who could see past the limitations of their own immediate context, and who were able to recognise the enormous achievement of Shakespeare as a poet, as a **creator of fascinating stage characters**, and as a writer who was able to breathe life into any and all aspects of human life, regardless of social class, moral righteousness, or lack thereof.

20th century

During the 20th century Shakespearian criticism finally blew up into a huge **area of research and analysis**. Efforts were made to examine Shakespeare's own contemporary world, socially, artistically and politically, which only served to enhance respect for his genius. Learning how to fix and identify Shakespeare within the

Richard III performed by German theatre company Schaubuehne Berlin at the Barbican Theatre, London (2017). © picture alliance/Photoshot

centuries-past environment of Elizabethan society and theatre, it was possible to paradoxically reveal for once and all **how important he was as a writer and poet**, and how universal and eternal his best work actually is. As noted by Kenneth Muir in his essay on Shakespeare's reputation through history, the people of the modern age (post-World War 2) "unconsciously find in Shakespeare what the modern age requires". Just like the Mona Lisa is said to keep her eye on you wherever you stand in relation to the painting, so too does Shakespeare never take his eye off us, and our messy and chaotic humanity.

5. MATERIALS

The Globe Theatre in London

The Elizabethan Age saw the first great flowering of the theatre in England. The theatre drew audiences from all social classes, and during the reign of Elizabeth I the theatres themselves became profitable enterprises and acting, for the first time, was a viable career.

Stage performances were very different from the theatre as we know it today. Lacking any kind of technical support, electricity or complex scenery, stage performances in Shakespeare's time took place during broad daylight (there being no way to artificially light a stage at night) and with extremely limited props and scenery. The actors carried the performance completely, with no support from special effects or elaborate backgrounds and props.

No women were allowed on stage

Another major difference between then and now was the fact that all roles on stage in the Elizabethan theatre had to be played by boys or men: no girls or women were allowed on stage. It was considered immoral or even blasphemous for women to participate in acting and theatrical events. So in the case of *Richard III*, we can assume that Lady Anne would have been played by a probably good-looking younger man or teenage boy, and old Queen Margaret by an older man.

Theatre was run by groups of writers-actors-producers; Shakespeare was a member of one of the so-called playing companies, called the Lord Chamberlain's Men (later the King's Men). It was the Lord Chamberlain's Men who built the original Globe Theatre in Southwark in London in 1599. Shakespeare was therefore writing his plays specifically for performance at the Globe. The original Globe was destroyed by fire in 1613, rebuilt in 1614 and then closed

This is what the Globe Theatre might have looked like at Shakespeare's time.
© picture alliance/Design Pics/Ken Welsh

The original Globe

by the authorities in 1642. A modern reconstruction was opened in 1997.

The original Globe was an amphitheatre with three storeys: that is, a semi-circle of three levels of seating for the audience curving around a stage surrounded by standing room at the ground level for the cheapest tickets. The whole structure was open air, with roofing over the rear of the stage area and over the uppermost terrace of seating. It is believed that the original Globe could hold an audience of 3,000.

The modern reconstruction (called *Shakespeare's Globe*) is as faithful to the original as possible given modern safety requirements (it has a maximum capacity of 1,500, for example). Performances at Shakespeare's Globe can provide modern audiences with at least an idea of what the theatre was like in Elizabethan times – more hygienic, less crowded, and with the inclusion of women on stage. As far as the optics, acoustics and physical arrangement is concerned, it's as close as can be to the original.

Shakespeare's Globe has proved to be incredibly popular since its opening in 1997, and now makes about £20 million per year. Plays are only performed on stage during the summer, but the playing company also tours the country with productions of Shakespeare's plays, and many productions are recorded for release on DVD.

Some useful information

Study *Richard III*

Any complete edition of *Richard III* will be usable when studying the play. Most editions include footnotes to help you understand the more arcane words and phrases in the text. Obviously, the act / scene / line breakdown should be the same in every edition.

The standard editions in the UK are the **Arden Shakespeare editions**, which all contain detailed footnotes and very useful essays on the context of each play and the historical / fictional sources Shakespeare used as source material. The Arden Shakespeare books are probably the best study editions available.

Another useful series is from the **Royal Shakespeare Company** (RSC). These editions are very easy to read (the pages are well laid-out and the print is clear and well-spaced) and contain less background / context information: these are the standard editions for actors preparing for the stage.

In Germany, there are several school book publishers with editions of the relevant plays. For this study guide we have used the Reclam edition.

There is beyond this no shortage of **secondary literature and reference material on Shakespeare**, who may be the most-written-about writer in world literature. Complete editions of his works (such as the *Oxford Shakespeare: The Complete Works*) will always have useful, brief introductions to each play, covering the circumstances of the play's writing, its general critical position within his works, and the themes and aspects of the play which make it interesting. Critical appreciation of Shakespeare and his works ebbs and flows like a tide, so it is also always rewarding to look at secondary literature and critical studies from less contemporary sources, e.g. essays and books from the 1950s.

Shakespeare

Al Pacino's *Looking for Richard*

The film itself (see also chapter 3.7 in this study guide, p. 89) is well worth hunting down if you are interested in the play or Shakespeare's lasting relevance. The following link is to a detailed and enlightening article / review about Pacino's film:
https://www.americanpopularculture.com/archive/film/pacino_shakespeare.htm (last accessed on 24.06.2020)

Looking for Richard

As usual, **Wikipedia** provides useful gateways into more detailed and varied sources for many topics. Particularly useful for *Richard III* are the genres (tragedy, history, Senecan tragedy, morality plays) which contribute to the finished play.

Wikipedia

6. SAMPLE EXAM QUESTIONS AND ANSWERS

Die Zahl der Sternchen bezeichnet das Anforderungsniveau der jeweiligen Aufgabe.

Here are some sample essay questions and responses. The number of stars indicates the level of difficulty of the task.

Task 1 **

Is Richard the hero or the villain of the play, and what other terms could be used to describe him?

Model answer:
A hero is, broadly, someone who overcomes obstacles on the way to doing good. This "good" will probably be something which benefits other people by removing problems or conquering enemies/bad situations.

A villain is someone who acts either only in their own interests (selfish) or who intentionally tries to bring harm and suffering down on other people (evil).

Richard, Duke of Gloucester, in Shakespeare's *Richard III* is obviously not a hero. In his own words, he is a villain (see I.1.30). His goals are absolutely selfish. He has no intention of taking the throne in order to bring peace and harmony – these are states of being he utterly rejects in his speech at the beginning of the play.

Abuse of power

He does conform to the general role of a villain. He is selfish and ambitious to the point of murder. Many of his acts are beyond any kind of moral justification, such as killing the young princes. Richard is evil: he is motivated by the selfish desire to have power and to use this power to crush anyone who opposes or even contradicts him.

But there is a specific word which describes Richard: protagonist. This is the main character in the play, "one who plays the first part" (the literal translation of the ancient Greek original). Richard is absolutely the villain, but he is also the central character, who completely dominates all other characters. So while Richard can be clearly classified as the villain in the play, he can and should be referred to as the protagonist, a literary term more suitable for a main character like Richard, no matter how heroic or villainous that character may be.

Central character in Richard III

Task 2 **

How are women portrayed in Shakespeare's play *Richard III*?

Model answer:
The women in *Richard III* are not treated well, by circumstances in the play or by their author, Shakespeare. Most of them are either widows (their husbands have been killed) or grieving mothers (their children have been killed). Richard's mother, the Duchess of York, in addition, is terribly ashamed for having given birth to such an evil creature. There are moments in the play where the women compare their grief and grievances, and at the end of it is always Richard and his murderous ambition. History and the story of the play treat these women very badly.

They also suffer at the hands of Shakespeare. He has written here female characters which are completely lacking in any significance beside their temporary usefulness to a male character. They can be married to establish connections to power, and then cast away

Women are powerless figures

or murdered when a new woman brings better connections. They have no power at all, with one exception: Old Queen Margaret has the power to curse, and her curses on Richard and his followers are recalled at many points throughout the play when they appear to be coming true.

But at the end of the day the women are not rounded characters at all, they serve functions within the plot for the author, and within the world of the play, they serve functions for the men around them. The women in *Richard III* have no "life" beyond their usefulness.

Task 3 **

Is Richard actually the only fully developed character in the play?

Model answer:

Richard is the main character in the play, he is the protagonist, and the villain at the same time. But unlike other complex characters in Shakespeare's plays, like for example the title character of *Hamlet* or the mad old king in *King Lear*, who are surrounded by shifting constellations of significant and well-formed characters, Richard essentially stands alone on stage.

> Stands alone on stage

He is without a doubt the only fully rounded character in the play. All other characters are only relevant in connection with him, whether they be loyalists (Buckingham) or opponents (Richmond). Everyone is moving around, put in motion by Richard's plotting and evil deeds. We get a vague impression of the personality of some of them – Clarence is naive and gullible, Hastings is complacent and unsuspecting, old Queen Margaret is eaten up with hatred and grief. But these and the other characters are all more like sketches surrounding the detailed, vibrant figure of Richard.

SOURCES & REFERENCES

Edition used for this study guide:
Geisen, Herbert: *William Shakespeare. King Richard III.* Reclam XL Englisch. Reclams Universal Bibliothek Nr. 19961. Ditzingen: Reclam jun. Verlag, 2019. → All page references are to this Reclam edition (Note: Act II Scene 4 lines 55–57 is written II.4.55–57)

Ohlmann, Pascal: *William Shakespeare. Richard III.* Berlin: Cornelsen Verlag, 2018.

Books about William Shakespeare's work:
Ford, Boris (ed): *The Pelican Guide to English Literature: The Age of Shakespeare.* Harmondsworth: Penguin Books, 1955.

Muir, Kenneth: *Changing Interpretations of Shakespeare.* In: Ford, Boris (ed.): The Age of Shakespeare. Harmondsworth: Penguin Books, 1955. pp. 282–301.

Wells, Stanley; Taylor, Gary (ed.): *William Shakespeare: The Complete Works.* Oxford: Oxford University Press, 1988.

→ Books like this – collections of academic essays covering different aspects of the work and environment of a writer or period – can be extremely useful for providing important context on contemporary details. The historical scene, the nature of humour on stage, the role of women, et cetera, are all things which are important for an understanding of the specific play, but are not available to us in black and white in the text of the play. A little research can be both fascinating and helpful when it comes to working with more difficult texts like Shakespeare's plays.

Guide to English Literature:

Greenblatt, Stephen; Abrams, M. H.: *The Norton Anthology of English Literature. Volume I.* New York, London: Norton & Company, 2006.

Seeber, Hans Ulrich (ed.): *Englische Literaturgeschichte*. Stuttgart: Metzler, 1991. → The histories of specific national literatures from Metzler Verlag are excellent resources. Organised thematically within a general chronological approach, they are ideal references for learning more about what came before whatever you are studying, providing succinct analyses of how literary movements or styles or techniques or materials develop and grow.

Online resources:

Wikipedia as always is a good place to start, and has entries for everything you might want to start looking at. It is important to remember that Wikipedia articles are not 100% reliable or suitable as citations. It is always worth making that little bit of extra effort to look at the references the articles provide and follow links to more substantial and stable original sources: → **www.wikipedia.de**

www.quoteinvestigator.com/2010/10/16/be-nice-on-way-up
→ Search for the origins of quotations

www.americanpopularculture.com/archive/film/pacino_shakespears.htm → About Al Pacino's film *Looking for Richard*

(Links last accessed on 24.06.2020)

INDEX

Aristotle 17
boar imagery 81, 85
Bosworth Field 7, 27, 39, 58
Catastrophe 7, 41, 42
Catharsis 17
Climax 7, 40
comedy 6, 16, 18, 19
curse 8, 26, 28, 29, 33, 37, 39, 51, 55, 57, 78, 79
Drake, Francis 12
Elizabethan Age 11, 13, 14, 18, 25, 88, 93, 94
Exposition 40
Falling action 7, 41
fate 42, 61, 64, 70, 77, 78
First Folio 10, 16, 20, 23
Freytag, Gustav 40
Globe Theatre 10, 94, 95
Green, Robert 10
Hall, Edward 23
Hildebrand, Theodor 36
history plays 6, 16, 19–21, 23, 24, 61, 62
Holinshead, Raphael 23
House of Lancaster 27, 43, 73
House of Tudor 6, 11, 24, 52, 54, 61, 64
House of York 24, 27, 43, 44, 73
inner monologue 81
Introduction 7, 40
irony 83
King James 14, 25
Looking for Richard 89, 97, 102
Lord Chamberlain's Men 10, 94
Lost years 9
Machiavelli, Niccoló 15
Marlowe, Christopher 11, 12, 14, 15, 61, 63
More, Thomas 23
Pacino, Al 89, 90, 97, 102
paranoia 7, 42, 46, 47, 78, 79
peripeteia 40
Queen Elizabeth I 11–13, 94
Queen Mary 11, 12
Renaissance 16, 21, 24
Resolution 7, 41, 42
rhetoric 25, 45, 51, 61, 78, 81
Rising action 7, 40
Seneca 16, 24
Senecan tragedy 24, 25
sonnets 16, 21
Spanish Armada 12, 13
supernatural elements 25, 39, 53, 60, 78, 80
tragedy 6, 16–18, 24, 40
Wars of the Roses 7, 20, 23, 27, 39, 42, 61

NOTICE